23

MY CRICKET DIARY '81

MY CRICKET DIARY '81

The West Indies, Australia, India

Graham Gooch
with Alan Lee

Stanley Paul
London Melbourne Sydney Auckland Johannesburg

Stanley Paul & Co. Ltd

An imprint of the Hutchinson Publishing Group

17–21 Conway Street, London W1P 6JD

Hutchinson Group (Australia) Pty Ltd
30–32 Cremorne Street, Richmond South, Victoria 3121
PO Box 151, Broadway, New South Wales 2007

Hutchinson Group (NZ) Ltd
32–34 View Road, PO Box 40-086, Glenfield, Auckland 10

Hutchinson Group (SA) Pty Ltd
PO Box 337, Bergvlei 2012, South Africa

First published 1982
© Graham Gooch 1982

Set in VIP Baskerville by
D. P. Media Limited, Hitchin, Hertfordshire

Printed in Great Britain by The Anchor Press Ltd
and bound by Wm Brendon & Son Ltd
both of Tiptree, Essex

British Library Cataloguing in Publication Data

Gooch, Graham
My cricket diary '81.
1. Cricket
I. Title   II. Lee, Alan
796.35′8′0924   GV913

ISBN 0 09 147750 6

Contents

DEDICATION

To the memory of
Ken Barrington

Introduction

Writing a book about a year in my cricket life may sound a straightforward operation; one sits down each evening and reflects on the events of the day, either with notes or by talking into a tape recorder. But in fact I found the experience both provocative and revealing, not to mention enjoyable.

It is sometimes all too easy to complete a day's cricket, or a match, and allow the incidents to slip into the recesses of memory, only to be dredged up at a pinch if someone happens to mention them in conversation. Sometimes, I confess, to forget has been a happy escape.

But in the preparation of this book, I have had to reflect more deeply on my own moods and emotions, observe others more closely and comment on them more carefully. Oddly enough, it has added a new dimension to the cricket routine.

Setting down the details, on and off the field, of a most remarkable year for me personally, and English cricket generally, has been a rewarding exercise, and I can only hope that the book produced by Alan Lee and myself gives as much pleasure as the cricket on which it is based.

Graham Gooch
January 1982

ACKNOWLEDGEMENTS

The author and publishers wish to thank
Adrian Murrell/All Sport for the use of
copyright photographs

1

Into Battle

Graham Gooch was the people's player of the year in 1980. His century against the West Indies at Lord's, vivid in colour and rich with strokes, had alone been enough to convert thousands to a talent which had simmered frustratingly beneath the surface since his premature Test baptism five years earlier. The fact that he also emerged as a character of considerable wit was an endearing bonus.

By the end of September the detached house in a tree-lined avenue near Romford, Essex, into which Graham and his wife Brenda had moved only a month previously, held a rapidly expanding collection of awards. But Gooch, who fits better than most into that over-used category, the family man, had by then temporarily switched off from cricket. England's first West Indies tour for seven years was not due to begin until mid-January and Gooch, a little jaded, intended to use the time wisely. His ambitions stretched no further than spending his evenings at home with Brenda and his days decorating their new home, playing golf and, given the chance, resuming his interrupted soccer playing. That chance arose in an unexpected manner which was ultimately to provide Gooch with his physical preparation for the rigours of the exacting tour ahead.

Chadwell Heath could have been a million miles from the Caribbean. I was there most days, in those cold, wet weeks that led up to Christmas, and my thoughts crossed the border between soccer and cricket only when someone brought up the subject of the coming tour. Pure chance had taken me, if only temporarily, into the West Ham training squad. Having grown up in that grey area between London's East End and the Essex countryside which is the Hammers' territory, I had followed them from boyhood. But since the demands of cricket had dictated a dramatic fall-off in my active football, the closest I had ever been to West Ham's players was the stand at Upton Park. Now, through a remark passed on by a friend of mine to John Lyall, the West Ham manager, I was sharing their facilities, their training routines and, up to a point, their lifestyle. The message had come back that, if I ever wanted to train there, I had only to phone and let John Lyall know. As the Chadwell Heath ground is only five minutes' drive from home the opportunity was too good to pass up, and before the end of November I was donning the training gear, the nylon tracksuits and boots, and sweating with the best of them.

As a method of getting physically prepared for the tour it was ideal. As a means of enjoyment for one whose love of playing football had long been frustrated it could not have been bettered. I trained as hard as the players, and surprised myself by coping quite adequately. I went whenever I possibly could and was accepted by the lads without a quibble, which emphasizes the mutual respect underlying any relationship between professional sportsmen. There is an indoor gymnasium at Chadwell Heath, plus an Astroturf all-weather pitch, a weight room and every other amenity I needed to get off the excess pounds. We had to weigh in once a week, and John Lyall set me a target. He promised me two tickets for their League Cup semi-final if I slimmed down to 13 stone from the 13 stone 10 lb at which I had started. I failed by 3 lb, but the incentive was a good one.

It might seem odd that I thought little about the tour ahead, for it was ostensibly the reason I was there. But I was so much enjoying the routine of training by day and relaxing by night that I really did not want to think ahead to the hard work that undoubtedly faced me in the Caribbean. For two and a half years I had played cricket virtually non-stop. That may not seem very long, but I had felt I wanted a complete break, to recharge my batteries and refresh my enthusiasm. I deliberately stayed at home most evenings, happy just to watch television and eat with Brenda after another summer of rarely being home before nine o'clock, even from a match at Chelmsford. At the same time I had no wish to be lazy about fitness. I frequently feel a better player when I know I am physically in trim – not technically, of course, but mentally. Sound in body, sound in mind is not a bad motto for an opening batsman who needs to remain alert and retain a high level of concentration over long periods. Even in the summer, when we play almost every day, I often run for a mile or so before play starts.

Once Christmas and New Year were past there was little time left before departure day. The usual pre-tour programme had to be undertaken, as well as a few commercial engagements which the team's agents had arranged for us. That apart, the routine was much the same as before my previous two England tours; only my nerves were worse. It is a common misconception that Test cricketers lose their nervousness as they gain in experience. I am not alone in feeling more tension before each successive series I play in. As I have established myself in the England team, and began to build a reasonable aggregate of Test runs, more and more has been expected of me. This is only natural from the public standpoint, but it inevitably inflicts more pressure. This tour was no exception. I read the papers and knew I had been named as one of England's best hopes of making challenging totals. I was flattered, but still nervous, and the tension was to stay with me until the tour was out of bottom gear, a few decent scores were under my belt and the Tests were upon us.

Leaving my wife and home is another thing which becomes harder every time. This year, with the tour starting so much later than usual, I had grown to enjoy my pattern of home life and it was a wrench to upset it. After two or three tours my early images of glamour had vanished. Like everyone else in the side I looked forward to the cricket, to the challenge of playing against the best side in the world. What I did not look forward to was the monotony of the off-field life. Until you have actually made a tour of three months or more it is impossible to appreciate the lifestyle. It is irritating, though perhaps understandable, when friends at home send you off with the words 'Have a good holiday', or 'Enjoy the sunshine, and think of us in the snow and ice at home.' What they can never realize is how many hours and days on every tour are spent feeling restless, bored, and in some cases very homesick.

Throughout the trip the squad lives in a cocooned world of its own. Decisions off the field are generally made for the players, who just have to be on time for meals, transport and practice. It all makes for tidy organization and leaves us free to concentrate exclusively on cricket, our reason for being there. But it does mean that life is nothing like as exciting as those at home believe. The greatest difficulty is occupying the mind, whether by reading, writing, sightseeing or simply sleeping. However stimulating the cricket may be, none of us can forget that our wives, girlfriends, and in some cases children are thousands of miles away.

If this sounds ungrateful, it is not intended. I am keenly aware of my good fortune in reaching the top of my profession and having the chance to be a celebrity in countries that many people pay a great deal of money just to visit. What I am trying to do is give an insight into the real life of the cricketer on tour, as opposed to the imagined one. Personally, I would reconsider my entire future if Brenda was not allowed to join me for part of each tour. The question of wives accompanying players has been discussed with considerable heat since long before my time as an England player. My view is that no one has the right to stop me paying for my wife to fly out to join me anywhere in the world. I can understand the argument that the players are there to do a job and should be free from distraction, but in my experience the comforting presence of his wife only does good to a cricketer under pressure.

For this trip, almost all the players had arranged for

14

their respective ladies to join them in Barbados, the liveliest and most pleasant of all the major centres. But that was not until mid-March, a very long way off as we gathered at Lord's on a bitterly cold Wednesday in January. Rain was slanting from a grey sky, snow was a distinct possibility, and the Caribbean suddenly seemed very inviting. The adrenalin began to flow as the traditional ceremonies of trying on tour uniforms, giving radio and television interviews and dressing for the eve-of-tour dinner went through with their customary clockwork efficiency.

Suddenly it was no longer some distant, intangible target. We were together, ready to go. In terms of past experience, we had a squad of players among whom only Brian Rose had never played in the Caribbean, yet only Geoff Boycott and Bob Willis had completed a full tour there with England or, as it then was, MCC. My own knowledge of the area extended to a fairly full tour with England Schools nine years earlier, and a fortnight in Barbados in 1979 playing for Vanburn Holder's benefit. I was well aware of the problems which could face us, particularly in the politically uncomfortable and reputedly violent cities of Kingston, Jamaica and Georgetown, Guyana, where – so everyone told me – one should never leave the hotel after dark. It was a harrowing prospect, so I turned my mind to cricket and trusted it might all be exaggeration.

What was clear from the outset was the good spirit within the party. We all knew each other from county, if not Test, cricket during the summer, and only Roland Butcher was touring with England for the first time. But it is strange how, in the confined atmosphere of the squad, one quickly finds out new things about team-mates. Take Graham Dilley: although he had been with us in Australia twelve months earlier, I knew him only as a quick bowler, a quiet man who had recently had glandular fever. By the time we reached Antigua, the island chosen for our week of acclimatization, I had learned that he was a keen player of the Space Invaders game – so fanatical that he had brought a miniature version of the game with him.

15

Naturally, sharing a room with someone brings you closer to them. I was down to share with John Emburey and quickly discovered that he had dreaded mosquitoes. In fact he went so far as to buy a device which, so the advertising claimed, attracted and killed all such insects. It comforted him, but did not cure his slight edginess every time he went to bed. One night we were both woken abruptly by a tremendous crash. I sat up violently, noticed the curtains blowing in through the window, and assumed we had an intruder. Embers was already out of bed, fearing the same. But all that had happened was the collapse of the air conditioning system on to the floor.

They treated us well in Antigua, and it was an ideal place in which to accustom one's body to the heat, and get in some good practice. It did not take long, however, to discover the existence of the *mañana* principle in the West Indies: when it comes to service in hotels, bars and restaurants, tomorrow really will do. When four of us went one day to the beach bar attached to our villas for a bite of lunch after nets we placed an order for tuna fish sandwiches. Fifteen minutes passed, then half an hour. The scenery was beautiful and the sunshine pleasant, but we were all hungry, so we were not pleased when the waitress returned empty-handed after exactly one hour. 'There is,' she informed us without a hint of remorse, 'no tuna fish.' This type of incident became commonplace, and we found the only thing to do was laugh – there was simply no point in getting annoyed. Alan Smith, our diplomatic manager, forced himself to adopt the same attitude in dealing with the shortcomings of the telephone service. In Trinidad, our second stop, it could take between two and six hours to place a call to London, and almost as long to phone one of the other islands.

Tranquil though it was in Antigua, most of us were pleased to move on to our opening match against the President's Young West Indies XI. The venue was Point-à-Pierre, a thirty-five-mile drive from our hotel at Port of Spain, but I was spared the slog and left, along with John Emburey, Paul Downton and Geoff 'Dusty'

Miller, to practise on a college ground in the capital each day. Bob Willis, as vice-captain, was also left out so that he could organize this practice. We drew lots to decide who would travel with the team as twelfth man each day; on the Friday, the first day of the game, Geoff Miller took the job. It was an odd stroke of fate, because without him England would possibly not have won the game. After looking at the wicket before play, Ian Botham and Alan Smith decided that it was likely to be more helpful to spin than to seam. So at the last possible moment Graham Stevenson was stood down and Dusty Miller took his place. He finished with nine wickets in the match as we won by 190 runs.

It was an encouraging way to start the tour, particularly so for David Gower. Cast by many as irresponsible when batting, he concentrated sternly for almost eight hours to score 187. It was not his prettiest innings, nor was it chanceless, but I am sure he obtained a great deal of satisfaction out of proving that he was far more than just casually talented. Geoff 'Fiery' Boycott began his trip with two scores of 87, and Mike Gatting, another whose detractors claim him to be incapable of a long innings, got his head down very capably to make 94.

By now, most of us had settled into the normal routine. When we were not playing a match, we would have breakfast around eight o'clock and leave for nets at about 9.30. The captain was exercising some discipline in this matter – lateness was punished by a fine, increasing at the rate of £1 per minute. I was caught for £2 very early on, but the man most troubled was David Gower. The only cure he could come up with to halt the decline in his finances was to put his watch on five minutes!

Following the victory in Trinidad, we flew north to the tiny holiday island of St Vincent. The airstrip is a matter of yards from the sea, but the cricket ground, next to it, is even closer. Wooded hills climb steeply away from the beach, along which run a series of villa-style hotels, our home for ten days. If you want nothing more than to lie on the beach, drink the local rum punch, plunge periodically into the sea to cool off and perhaps take a boat across to Mustique, island of the Beautiful People, you would love St Vincent. For professional cricketers trying to conduct an international tour it had severe drawbacks.

The first problem to blight our stay – though we could hardly blame the island for it – was the weather. It began to rain on our second day there, and failed to stop for the next forty-eight hours. The effect was disastrous. The opening two days of our scheduled first-class match against the Windward Islands were totally washed out; our management, seeking to make the best of a poor job, substituted two one-day games on the remaining days. That might have been bearable but for the second difficulty, the complete lack of adequate net facilities. Those provided for us on the edge of the square would do a practising batsman far more harm than good – the ball bounced inconsistently, some balls leaped around your ears, and others turned alarmingly. I felt sorry for Brian Rose, who had been out for nought to the third ball of the tour in Point-à-Pierre and was now trying to rebuild form and confidence. He came out of the net looking unhappier than when he went in. The only other net on the island took us from the sublime to the ridiculous. It was a concrete strip, about half the length of a cricket pitch, laid in what was nothing better than a cow patch. Fiery Boycott, whose attitude to daily netting verges on the religious, organized himself there with a troop of locals to bowl at him. Cows, goats and pigs looked on curiously at one of the oddest scenes on an England tour for many years.

Opening partners though we are, there are few similarities in attitude to nets between Boycott and myself. He does not feel happy unless he has a knock every day, and he obviously gets enormous benefit from it, but I am content with an occasional net to brush up some point of my game. In England I very rarely net at all during a season with Essex, probably because there have never been permanent off-field nets at Chelmsford, so I have grown up at the club doing without them. Even on the day before a Test, along with certain others such as David

Gower I prefer just to have a few balls thrown for me in a quiet corner rather than go through a complete net. It is purely a matter of choice – unfortunately on St Vincent there was no choice. It might sound ungracious to be critical of a small island's facilities, but since they had known we were coming for a long time there should have been no problem in providing at least one decent net.

My other predominant memory of St Vincent was boredom. Again, I can imagine the sceptical response to such a claim from those who were slogging their way to work at the same time through snow and slush in an English winter. But it is very difficult to occupy oneself on such a sleepy island when it is pouring with rain. I found myself going to bed by 9.30 on most nights.

We won both the limited-overs matches, the first by 16 runs and the second by six wickets. They were useful warm-ups against moderate opposition, and by making 50 in the second match I at least felt a little more confident. It was far too early, however, to make any self-judgements. The one-day international on the island was only two days away and I had played two innings in what were the equivalent of the friendlies Essex might play before starting the first-class season at home. The first of these two games provided two notable incidents, both of them involving Bob Willis. It was Bob's first bowl of the tour and he picked up his opening wicket in amusing style as the West Indians' opener, Sebastian, decided to give him the charge. It was not just a controlled advance down the pitch; he was on his horse with his bugle out. Bob saw him coming, dug the ball in short and, characteristically, marched briskly back with some satisfaction as the delivery bit, took off steeply, and lobbed gently off a thrown-up glove to be caught at slip. Sadly, Bob was still seeking his most fluent rhythm when his left foot caught in an old foothold, and the knee with which he has had so much trouble in the past twisted painfully. He limped off for treatment, took no further part in the match, and did not play again until after the First Test.

The first of the one-day internationals, scheduled for

Wednesday, 4 February, was preceded by two official team functions on successive nights. Players are rightly expected to attend a number of these parties on a West Indies tour, just as in any other country, and they can be relaxing and enjoyable. But usually no social demands are made on the players the night before an important match. On this occasion, however, we had to endure a twenty-minute drive along unmade roads, cramped together like sardines in the minibus which had been our means of transport throughout the stay in St Vincent. Once there, we found the company was almost identical to that at the previous night's function and, much as we were made to feel welcome, none of us did more than sip orange juice and sit together in corners of the house. While appreciating the hospitality of our hosts – in this case the president of the local cricket association – I felt it was an unwise precedent to set.

We lost the international by the gallingly narrow margin of two runs, exactly the same result we had suffered in a similarly tense finish against the West Indies at Melbourne a year earlier. It was disappointing, certainly, but it did us no harm to come so close, especially after our lack of real preparation. One-day internationals never compare with Tests for importance – certainly not in the minds of the players – and with only two of them punctuating this tour they were just regarded as showpieces.

We drove down the narrow lane which approaches the ground and borders the airfield at 8.30 a.m., ninety minutes before the scheduled start. We had heard any number of fanciful estimates of the crowd, from 5000 to 25,000, though it would have been physically impossible to accommodate 25,000. Even at that early hour the quaint little ground was alive: early, ticketless invaders were scrambling up the walls and fences and the whole scene was full of colour.

Ian Botham won the toss and elected to bowl first, extracting during the morning session any dampness there might have been in the wicket. We hoped for a few quick wickets, but dreamed of nothing as sensational as the

20

lunch score of 110 for seven. Our bowling was tidy, the fielding was good, and when I was brought on I decided to experiment by bowling cutters instead of my usual gentle swing. It worked to the extent that I took two for 12 in six overs, and this persuaded me that I should adopt cutters for the rest of the tour. The theory behind this change of style was that the shine comes off the ball very quickly on the coarse outfields of the Caribbean, making it very difficult to sustain any swing. On wickets which are generally slow and sometimes bounce unevenly, I found I could cut the ball either way and that the odd one would 'stop' or lift sufficiently to disturb the batsman. We were playing on the same pitch that had seen service for the previous two games, and from the outset the ball also turned for the spinners. I was left wondering just what sort of pitch we would have had if the four-day match had gone through as planned!

A target of 128 should have been well within our compass, even against the best pace attack in the world and on a difficult pitch; but after Fiery and I had gathered 14 from the first six overs we suddenly lost four wickets for one run. If it was not total disaster, we were at least making things very hard for ourselves. I was out to a bad ball, playing at one well wide of off-stump from Andy Roberts. But it was Colin Croft, cutting the ball at high speed, who took the other three early wickets, and indeed went on to win them the game with figures of six for 15. Ian and David Gower both played well to put on 65, and at 80 for four we were back in a winning position. Funnily enough, as I sat on a bench outside the dressing-room I always thought we would win, even if it meant batting through to the last of the 50 overs to do so. I was proved wrong as first Croft and then Michael Holding returned with the crucial spells to see off our lower order. Botham was eighth out with only 14 more runs needed, but in a frantic finish we missed out, and could only look on dejectedly as thousands of dancing, delirious locals poured on to the ground.

We hardly had time to sulk about the defeat. Within

half an hour we were whisked away in that minibus – 'The Blinking Bus', as its owner had aptly painted over the windscreen – for introductions to the Prime Minister. No one could have accused us of slinking off in ill humour, for we mixed with the locals at two further functions that night and retired not long before our pick-up time of 6 a.m. Originally we had been scheduled to fly out on a civilized mid-morning flight. This dawn flight, substituted at a few hours' notice, gave the manager further anxiety but hardly surprised the players. It was merely an appropriately confused finale to a stay which had done little to advance our preparations for the series to come. Worse was to follow, because the flight switch had come too late for anyone to inform the relevant people in Trinidad. So when we arrived at breakfast time, we found no transport. Bernard Thomas, our physiotherapist, led an advance party by taxi back to the Hilton, a forty-five-minute drive away, and the rest of us slumped in an undignified, exhausted heap in the airport lounge. Some slept, some tried to read, and all became a little irritable. Ninety minutes later we were finally rescued. Lashing rain caused us to abandon any thoughts of an afternoon practice, and most of us took the chance to catch up on some sleep.

The rain returned two days later, just in time to wash out the opening day of our game with Trinidad after only twenty-one deliveries. Deryck Murray, Trinidad's captain, had put us in to bat, and Fiery and I knew our batting time would be short-lived as we watched the clouds roll towards us over the hills which rose spectacularly behind the Queen's Park Oval.

When the rains relented, the following day, I scored 117. Playing in a live situation for most of a day left me feeling far more content, but in truth it counted for little as a warm-up for the Test, now less than a week away. Trinidad's attack was led by the gentle medium pace of Larry Gomes, who used to bowl second change for Middlesex, and neither he nor his new-ball partner were very frightening on a slow, low pitch. For the only time on tour

22

we faced three spinners – all of them very capable – and I found it stimulating to revert to this type of contest. I batted without a helmet for the first time in twelve months, and felt composed and confident. Fiery and David Gower also made runs, but poor Brian Rose missed out again. Number three had become a problem position, and no one needed to remind Rosey of that. All sorts of names were being suggested to fill that role in the Test team, but my own feeling was that we should stand by someone who had done the job regularly.

Even on a wicket such as Trinidad, where the ball seldom bounces above stump height, the quicker bowlers are dangerous. I noted here that getting on the back foot, even against someone of Gomes' pace, was perilous, because the occasional delivery was liable to shoot through very low. Naturally, the quicker the bowler, the more hazardous this becomes for the batsmen. But there was little chance of the ball swinging or seaming after the opening few overs, because within an hour of the start it resembled a well-used lump of suede. That was a problem encountered by Graham 'Picca' Dilley on the third day of this game, and he allowed it to discourage him more than he should. He can be moody, and the lack of response as he banged the ball into the pitch left him quite visibly depressed. The situation ended in a stand-up argument with the captain, who threw up his arms, clapped his hands and promptly took Picca off. It was an affair that flashed and then died in the heat of a very swift moment, but the press made much of it. My own impression is that Picca, more than any other England bowler, needs gentle encouragement to bring him out – and that he must learn that he will not make the ball fly every time he comes on.

2

Shape of Things to Come

Even in their darkest moments, the players in the England tour party could not have imagined a worse launch to the Caribbean series than that which befell them at Port of Spain's Queen's Park Oval. They were beaten by an innings and 79 runs, and in a manner which, if cricket had any affinity to logic, would surely have precluded any prospects of reversing the form. Twice, in appreciably less than three days, they were bowled out for under 200 by the West Indian pace quartet of Andy Richards, Mike Holding, Colin Croft and Joel Garner.

To make matters much worse, captain Ian Botham had said, in a moment of reckless bravado on the rest day, that there was '. . . no way we can lose this game – and a few heads will roll if we do'. It was a typical Botham statement, full of well-intended aggression, but in the circumstances disastrously misguided. By the end of the match it was being compared as a catchphrase to that infamous 'We can make them grovel' remark by Tony Greig, when captain against the same opposition in 1976. Defeat, and the nasty taste it left in the mouth, could have one of two consequences. Either the squad would emerge hardened and improved by the experience, or a process of fragmentation would begin.

All this, however, had seemed safely remote in the days which led up to the match. Team headquarters was the Hilton Hotel, tucked into a hillside overlooking the oil-rich city of Port of Spain as it prepared for its annual carnival. Every day, hundreds of locals jogged and exercised around the vast green savannah, simply to get fit enough for the rigours of carnival – three solid days of no sleep but plenty of rum. Inside the hotel, the already dilatory service faded significantly. The pharmacy and newsagent's stall in the lobby

24

*opened more than an hour late – 'Because it's carnival, man –
everyone's high!' – and room service ground nearly to a halt. But a
disruptive element of a quite different and much more serious nature
was awaiting the players as they prepared for their first stern cricket
examination of the trip.*

We saw the placards as we drove into the ground for nets,
two days before the start of the Test. The words were
misspelt and the message poorly expressed, but the feelings of the local guys carrying them were plain enough –
Deryck Murray, captain of Trinidad and their island idol,
had been left out of the West Indies team and they
intended to make a fuss about it. There were no more than
half a dozen demonstrators there that morning, but we
had only to read the Trinidad papers to get a clearer idea
of the extent of local indignation. Front-page pictures,
cartoons and editorial comment all broadened the issue
out of all proportion, until it was not surprising that local
cricket followers began to feel militant.

It was my first experience of such nationalistic fervour.
It is not something I can imagine ever happening in
England – although there have been instances of crowds,
notably in Yorkshire, voicing their disapproval of a local
man's omission from an England side – but in the West
Indies, and especially Trinidad, it is apparently as perennial as carnival. What we could not have guessed at that
point was the effect that it was to have on the Test. Later
that same day it gathered momentum with a boycott by
Trinidadians of the pre-series West Indies Board Dinner
at the Holiday Inn in Port of Spain. At first none of us
could understand why three tables stood conspicuously
empty, but when someone explained it all fell into place.

That same evening we heard that anonymous phone
calls had been received by the ground authority, threatening to dig up the pitch. An extra, all-night guard was
posted on the wicket, and floodlights erected. Surely, we
thought, it was all a hoax anyway? Since the George Davis
protest of 1975, when the Headingley pitch was vandal-
ized by demonstrators seeking Davis' release from prison,

nothing similar had occurred. I could not believe that support for a thirty-seven-year-old wicketkeeper, who probably admitted himself past his best, could go to such extremes. How wrong can you be! The row rumbled on the following morning in the papers, which contained various letters urging a boycott of the match. But by now we were all too concerned with our own preparations to pay much attention.

As often happens in England these days, both teams were staying in the same hotel, and we met most of the opposition for the first time on Thursday morning, the day before the game. Not that many of the faces were new to us – the majority of the West Indies side have played county cricket in England, so there is a familiarity between our two teams which does not exist elsewhere on the Test circuit. Nevertheless, I am not convinced it is ideal for the players of both sides to be on top of each other. However well we may get on socially, awkward moments can occur before and during Tests.

Our Test twelve was publicly announced at breakfast time on Thursday – the players themselves had been told the previous day. The press, naturally enough, seized upon two newsworthy selections – Brian Rose had kept his place at number three despite his lack of form, and Paul Downton, who would be making his Test début, was chosen ahead of David 'Blue' Bairstow as wicketkeeper. Blue had been injured for the previous match, and Paul had taken his chance well, but there was a general feeling that Paul might have been preferred anyway as the better of the two keepers at standing up to spinners.

Poor facilities and unkind weather had not made our practice efforts on the tour go smoothly, so it was with more resignation than annoyance that we accepted yet another disruption at nets that morning. This time a heavy shower left the net surfaces unplayable and sent us back to the Hilton feeling frustrated once again. As usual the day before a Test, the remaining daylight hours were left free – although it goes without saying that no one does anything too strenuous. After a couple of hours sitting by the hotel pool with Ian Botham and his Somerset mate Viv Richards I felt in need of some exercise, just to shake the lethargy out of my system. So Dusty Miller and I set off for a twenty-minute run around the savannah, returning in time for a shower before the rituals of Test match eves began.

Most youngsters coming into Test cricket for the first time fail to grasp the importance of the team meeting and dinner which precede every Test. I'm sure I was no different, but now I fully appreciate the importance of getting everyone together, establishing a togetherness, and of course discussing the relative merits and weaknesses of the opposition. On tour, the team meeting, traditionally, begins around 6.15 in the manager's suite, the living part of which is always converted into a team room where players can come at any time for a drink and a chat. No one else, not even the players' friends or the travelling press, is allowed into that sanctum. We sat in casual clothes, with a glass of beer or a soft drink, and the captain as usual stood up first. This was to be a vital match for Ian Botham. It was his first Test abroad as captain and he needed to make an impression, if only to rid himself of those who had criticized him during the unsuccessful summer series against the West Indies.

It was a good, motivating speech, impressing his authority on us for perhaps the first time on the tour. If there was a criticism of Ian within the team – and it was not one we kept from him – it was that he treated all players the same, without delving deeper to find out what made each individual tick. His words at this first, crucial meeting of the trip encouraged us all. We analysed each member of the West Indies team, discussing how best to bowl and set fields to them, or, in the bowlers' cases, how best to play them. This was not something we would repeat before every Test, since the players would not alter dramatically, but before the first match of a series it was valid and useful, especially for those who had not toured before and had not attended such a meeting.

The major disagreement arose over Richards. Ian

27

believed that we should set an attacking field when he
came in, just as we had always done and as we would do
for any other player. But Bob Willis, still injured and out
of the game, put forward the theory that we should spread
the field deep immediately and make Viv work for every
run. Bob, more than anyone else, knew just how devastating Viv could be. At Old Trafford during the 1980 series
he had bowled a moderate but by no means generous
spell, and Richards had simply taken him apart, scoring
30 to 40 in two or three overs. It was savage stuff and it
obviously set Willis' keen cricket brain thinking. His conclusion was that if we defended, and stopped Viv picking
up the early boundaries, he might just become frustrated
and do something silly. It was also decided, quite logically,
to put extra pressure on the new West Indian batsman,
Everton Mattis. Although he had made runs against us at
Point-à-Pierre, and again in the St Vincent international,
a Test début was bound to stretch his nerves, and close
fielders would do nothing to comfort him.

In the general discussion, I noticed that those with
something to say were generally the experienced Test
players – Ian, Bob, Geoff Miller and myself – but that the
man with by far the most experience, Geoffrey Boycott,
said nothing at all. He just made notes, for what purpose I
wasn't sure. When asked if he had anything to add, he
simply said he was interested in everyone else's views – a
noticeable lack of helpful opinion from one about to start
his ninety-fifth test.

Ian and Alan Smith broached the subject of possible
crowd trouble and stressed that everyone should stay
calm. If any bottles or other objects were thrown on to the
playing area, those in the target zone should not make a
fuss, but walk into the middle and report to the umpires.
John Emburey remarked drily that if anyone threw a
bottle at him he would seek permission to run, rather than
walk.

It was a full and frank meeting, but which I felt had one
regrettable omission: nothing was said about who was to
be twelfth man. In different circumstances I could have

28

understood it, for very often the choice hangs between a batsman and a bowler, or between two different types of bowler, and rests on the state of the wicket just before the game. But on this occasion we all knew that it would be a batsman who stood down and that only two men, Peter Willey and Mike Gatting, were in contention. I thought it would have been fairer to them both to make the decision known at the meeting. The second part of a pre-match evening is like a sedative following a stimulant. Everyone has their thoughts pinned on the match ahead, so the dinner offers informal relaxation for an hour or so, during which the match is seldom discussed. On this occasion it was even more light-hearted than usual, and the assistant manager, Ken Barrington, was the target for a hilarious prank devised by Graham Dilley. The background to the joke was this. Our transport in Trinidad, supplied and paid for by the West Indies Board, consisted of taxis which proved neither reliable or punctual. After a number of missed appointments and late arrivals 'Colonel' Barrington had developed a complex about Battu Bros, the taxi firm in question, and was forever phoning them up to confirm arrangements. On the night before the game the Colonel was particularly jumpy as we wanted to leave for the ground earlier than usual, at 8.30 the following morning. So when the phone rang just as coffee was being served he expected the worst, and got it. He was told that two of Battu's taxis had been involved in an accident, and that they would be able to provide only one vehicle at the booked time. Kenny was blissfully unaware that he had been talking to Graham Dilley. A few moments later came another call. Battu could not manage 8.30 but could provide two cabs at 7.45. Kenny, chuckling at this disorganized state of affairs but not particularly surprised and certainly not suspicious, reported the news to the team. That time he had been talking to David Bairstow.

Over the next twenty minutes six further calls were made, all fielded by Kenny, and all claiming to be Battu Bros with tales of woe, which reached a peak when they claimed they could send a minibus but that it needed a few spares fitted . . . like a steering wheel. Picca and Blue had both slipped out to the lobby to make second calls, and David Gower and Roland Butcher took their turn. Each time someone went out, ostensibly to go to the lavatory, his place at the table was filled by everyone moving across a few inches; so even when Kenny became aware of that he was possibly being conned he could spot no one missing when he glanced around. Ironically, the voice he finally recognized was that of Roland Butcher, the one man among us who could talk in a local accent without straining a vocal muscle! Kenny, as expected, took the prank in great spirit and everyone departed in good humour.

The match was now a matter of twelve hours away, and I went to bed thinking realistically about our chances. I knew, as we all did, that our best hope lay with our spinners. But if they were to have the scope to do their job we first had to make enough runs – 400 or 450. Against the best attack in the world, a series of shock bowlers who might run through any batting order but had the secondary ability to keep things tight, I did not kid myself. We were the underdogs all right, and at pretty long odds too.

I slept as well as usual. Some players, particularly Bob Willis, find sleeping on the eve of a Test particularly difficult, but I have not had any problems since the natural nerves of my first few England games. I woke around seven as usual, and breakfasted in the restaurant half an hour later. There is a noticeable tension on the first morning of any Test – the jokes become a little strained, and the talk rarely strays naturally from the match in hand. It was no different this time. The taxis, thankfully, did arrive on time and in appropriate force. We left so early because word had reached us that the West Indies were due to depart for the ground at nine. By bringing forward our time by half an hour we guaranteed ourselves the net facilities, although as things turned out it was of no account, since the West Indies were content to have their knock-up and exercise routine on the outfield.

From their selected thirteen they left out Faoud Bacchus and Ranjie Nanan. The choice was predictable,

30

leaving all four quick bowlers in the side, and it became something of a standing joke in our side that poor Nanan had only been included because he was a Trinidadian – the crowd would be pleased, and as twelfth man he would at least know where the drinks were kept! England's twelfth man was Mike Gatting, although that had still not been announced an hour before the start when I and several other players went out to look at the wicket.

It had rained heavily during the night, so when we saw at one end a wet patch, about a yard square and just short of a length, I assumed it had been caused by a leak in the covers. Further on, past the far end of the pitch from the pavilion, we discovered what can only be described as a bog where the quick bowlers would be reaching the climax of their run-up. It was apparently caused by a drain. That, and the wet patch on the wicket, would ensure a delayed start.

At that stage it occurred to none of us even to wonder whether the pro-Deryck Murray demonstrators had been at work. Hadn't there been a guard on the ground all night? And wasn't it also protected by a floodlight system? The idea would have seemed absurd. It was not until after lunch that we were officially told the truth. The pitch had been sabotaged during the night: vandals had cut a hole in the covers, then dug out a section of the wicket. It had been discovered by the ground staff when they reported for duty, and their cure was to fill the hole with wet mud and roll it in – hence the wet patch. The guard had apparently not turned up, which seemed highly convenient for the saboteurs, and the floodlights had been smashed.

Even Alan Smith, our manager, was kept in the dark until past lunchtime. He is the most diplomatic of men, but confessed himself 'rather surprised' not to be told any earlier. As a team, we were left to find out for ourselves. And the crowd? They did not have a clue what had happened – a situation exploited by the locals and which very nearly sparked an unpleasant riot. As far as the paying public in the stands and terraces knew, the sun was shining and they should be watching cricket. If only an

31

announcement had been made that vandals had tam-
pered with the pitch they might have accepted the delay,
but there was nothing. So as the afternoon wore on 15,000
people grew steadily more restless.

Eventually the captains – both unwilling to start with
conditions as they were – came under heavy pressure from
the ground authority. It is not the first time this has
happened and I doubt if it will be the last, even if it does
smack of officials trying to save their necks at the expense
of the players. Basically, the cover-up had gone on too
long. The crowd had been there for four hours waiting for
some action, and as time went by the chances of them
swallowing a claim that the wicket was unfit due to van-
dalism had diminished. Even if the truth had been told at
2 p.m., I think the crowd would have been sceptical.

So the captains were over-ruled. Play had to start – and
only just in time, as it turned out. Even as the two skippers
met at the top of the pavilion steps and prepared to walk to
the middle for the toss, bottles and cans began to shower
down on the outfield from the jeering, hooting crowd. The
missiles and the noise grew as Ian Botham and Clive
Lloyd approached the ground. Twenty yards from the
wicket they stopped. Ian flung his arms wide, and it was
obvious what they were saying. Watching from the
dressing-room, I silently urged them to carry on; the
crowd, already hostile and shouting abuse at us all, would
have gone berserk otherwise.

Ian won the toss and put the West Indies in to bat. It
was the only thing he could do in the conditions, and I'm
certain Lloyd would have done the same. If wickets get wet
for any reason, they often give unnatural life to the quicker
bowlers. Not only did we want to have that advantage for
our attack, but we certainly did not want our batting at
such risk from their four fast men. As it turned out we got
virtually no help from the pitch, which was extremely
disappointing. Graham Dilley bowled encouragingly fast
and well without much luck, and in the less than three
hours' play which remained that night Gordon Greenidge
and Desmond Haynes put on an unbroken 144 for the first

wicket. That was worse than it sounds, for it meant that with four days left we already had almost no chance of winning. Unless we bowled them out very fast on the second day – and nothing had indicated that it was remotely possible – the most we could hope for was a draw.

Not surprisingly, the team room that evening was not a lively place, and most of us left pretty quickly for a quiet meal and drink and an early night. Saturday, thankfully, was free from saboteurs and provided us with our highest moments of the game. We contained their batsmen to 221 runs in six hours and picked up seven wickets – five of them falling to John Emburey, who bowled his off-spinners for all but an hour of the day, 40 overs in all.

At first the policy was simply to keep things tight. Embers tempted Greenidge out quite early on, but a few minutes before lunch they were 203 for one and not in any visible trouble. Looking back on those closing overs reminds me of a saying of Geoff Boycott's: whatever your total, add on two wickets and see how it looks. Haynes was the first of the two to go, superbly caught and bowled by Emburey, who then picked off Mattis – caught at short leg while under pressure from a close-set field, just as we had discussed two nights earlier.

They went into lunch at 204 for three, with Richards still there but unhappy at his failure to pierce the deep-set field we had adopted on Bob Willis' advice. After the break, his frustration increased. Both Ian and Embers bowled well at him and once, while standing at silly point, I heard him curse violently as he slogged the off-spinner just over mid-wicket. We were getting through to him – the plan was working. And very quickly it brought complete success as he mistimed a pull at a short ball from Geoff Miller and gave David Gower a simple catch at square leg. Larry Gomes hung around for a long while, scoring only five, before Chilly Old got him with the new ball, at which point they were five down for 257. After the unhappy position in which we had begun the day we were now understandably pleased with ourselves.

The sixth-wicket stand which pulled the innings round was between the captain, Lloyd, and the wicketkeeper, David Murray. What an irony! Clive, who had been accused of discrimination in team selection issues, had been abused in the nets by Trinidadians and was now booed noisily as he came on to bat; and the Barbadian Murray was booed simply because he had been good enough to gain selection ahead of the Trinidadian Murray. The crowd did not know whether to cheer or not as these two put on 75. Both of them were in some discomfort as Dilley bowled a really fine spell in mid-afternoon. He dug in the occasional ball to make even the great Clive Lloyd hop about, and was generally as quick as anyone else in the game.

Dilley came off, unluckily without a wicket, and back came Embers for another marathon spell. He dismissed both Lloyd and Murray before the close, despite having to bowl in his sunglasses because of the glare from the setting sun. There had been a moment of humour during tea as he loudly inquired if anyone had any knicker elastic to hold his glasses on, and another on the field when I shouted, 'Bowler's name?' from slip as this bespectacled figure prepared to deliver. But for all that he gave a magnificent performance. For anyone to bowl 40 overs in a day requires a massive effort of concentration. His line and length seldom wavered, and his composure never slipped at all. If there is a better off-spinner in modern Test cricket I have yet to see him.

Sunday, for reasons unconnected with cricket, was the rest day – though 'rest' appeared to be the last thing that Port of Spain had in mind for us. The terrace and pool area of our hotel were taken over for the entire day by a West Indian 'fête', which comprised two brass bands blasting at full volume and a great deal of rum. If you left the hotel and escaped down the hill towards the town, you could just get out of earshot of the brass bands before hearing another driving beat from the savannah, where no less than fifty-six steel bands were engaged in a contest lasting all day and well into the night. Faced with such opposition to peace and quiet I was among a group of players who set off in a motor launch to explore the tiny islands off Trinidad's coastline. We returned at six in time for the brass bands' finale, and I went to bed almost immediately, knowing that the innings I was to play the following day could be among the most important of the tour.

If we were to save the game, we needed first to pick up the last three wickets quickly, and then to bat well through the rest of the day. As it turned out we achieved neither objective, and ended day three with the follow-on staring us in the face. The first hour was embarrassing, as the West Indies tail added 61 runs and left Clive Lloyd with the smug luxury of declaring at 426 for nine. Andy Roberts, who can be one of the best sloggers in the game on his day, limbered up for his bowling stint with an unbeaten half-century, including one devastating over of hitting at the expense of Ian Botham. Twenty-four runs came from five deliveries – the sequence was four-six-two-six-six – and much as the crowd lapped it up it represented a disastrous few minutes for our chances.

We came off the field disappointingly down, because after such a good second day we had let it all slip away from us and now faced a formidable battle to stay in the game. We began well enough. Michael Holding couldn't get himself right, and Fiery and I, both playing with freedom, scored 45 at a run a minute up to lunch. That, sadly, was about the highest point of our innings. Boycott, perhaps disturbed by a very good bouncer from Croft, followed the next ball outside off-stump and was caught at third slip. Two deliveries into the afternoon and we had lost our most experienced player! Brian Rose came in and was soon weaving as Croft fired two vicious short balls past his nose: the old familiar story.

My rush of pre-lunch strokes had dried up and, although I felt secure enough, I found I could not score a run. I told myself that it didn't matter, that we had no chance of winning, and that my job was simply to stay there at all costs; but being the player I am I dislike being

35

bogged down. The bowler who really frustrated me was Joel Garner. You could argue for hours about the relative merits of the four West Indian pacemen, but ask me who I would choose first in my side and I will say Garner every time. Even in the darkest crisis, I am not the type to push back a half volley defensively – but Garner just wore me down because he simply never bowled one. I batted through that entire two-hour session for just 17 runs, and I cannot remember ever having scored so few in a similar time. Just before tea Garner seemed to decide he could remove me with a yorker, and promptly bowled three in succession. The first rapped me on the bottom of the pad and must have been very close to l.b.w.; the second knocked flat all three stumps but was a no-ball; the last was a full pitch and I had so lost my touch that I hit it straight at mid-on.

Croft bowled from the other end for much of the afternoon and troubled every batsman, partly due to his wide angle of delivery and partly because he can bowl leg-cutters at very high speed. In England I have never worried about Croft because he has tended to bowl too short, but here he was a different proposition. He kept the ball well up, and goaded me into playing at balls which were really wide enough to leave alone. In the end it was neither Croft nor Garner who dismissed me, but Roberts. He returned to the attack after tea and bowled me 'through the gate' with one which nipped back off the pitch to beat my hesitant forward stroke. I had scored 41 painstaking runs, but I reasoned that those runs might well prove invaluable if we had a close call later in the game. Just as important as my score was the time I had occupied the crease – more than three hours. I had never before scored as slowly – not even against this cramping attack.

When you lose one wicket against the West Indians there is always the danger of an avalanche, and that is what happened now. Four more went in the time remaining that night – two wickets each for Croft and Garner – and by stumps we were 159 for seven and still an eternity away from saving the follow-on. Our one real hope seemed to lie with David 'Lulu' Gower, who had come in at the fall of Rose's wicket at 2.10 and batted through to the close with a great deal of discipline. I had been impressed with the way he had played already on the tour. This confirmed his improvement, which stemmed mainly from a new awareness of his previous faults and a willingness to concentrate for long periods. He has always been a high-class stroke player; now, it seemed , he was maturing into a genuine Test match batsman. We badly wanted him to bat through until lunch the next day, but in fact he survived only two overs. Croft had him l.b.w., and with that we were condemned to follow on. John Emburey added some obstinate batting to his earlier achievements in this game, and a spot of rain did us no harm, but the new ball finished us off and Fiery and I had to go out and start again only twenty-four hours after our first effort began.

This time we encountered a very different Holding. Totally overshadowed in the first innings, he now rushed in with great hostility, as if determined to confirm his reputation as the world's quickest bowler. He was able to skid the ball through off a surface which had become a little damp, and in his fifth over he beat me for pace through the air and I was gone, l.b.w. for five. Fiery has told me in the past that, against this West Indian attack, you have to accept that you will be cleaned up for very few runs about once in every three innings: they are as good as that. Until you have been batting for half an hour or more and feel really in, you move on to the back foot mechanically. The textbook, which teaches batsmen to pick the flight before moving their feet, is useless, because these bowlers are so quick you simply don't have time to wait. It is rather like a goalkeeper facing a penalty. Officially, he is not permitted to move his feet until the ball is kicked – but how many apply that regulation strictly? They decide which way to dive and they go, because to wait for the kick is to concede the goal.

In that same new-ball spell Holding took his hundredth Test wicket, poor Rosey being the victim. We were 25 for two, still 223 behind, and we had all played long enough to know what that meant. Psychologically, as well as numerically, we were in a mess. The bowlers, with runs to spare, could attack with enthusiasm and no worries. And however hard our side might have tried to play normally and just concentrate on staying there, it was in the back of everyone's mind that we were following on, and walking along a tightrope with no safety net. Fiery and Lulu Gower fought it through to the end of the day. Boycott was in his element, thriving on the challenge of survival and neither expected nor wanted to play strokes. Gower impressed me again, surviving the odd alarm and keeping his head splendidly. But, having been unbeaten overnight twice in succession, David was out almost as early on the fifth day as he had been on the fourth. He had shared a stand of 61, precious but not enough to save us. From then on the wickets fell steadily, and the match ended in a clatter of four wickets for six runs. We had lost by an innings and 79 runs, with slightly more than an hour to spare, on a last day most remarkable for a marvellous knock by Fiery and an awful piece of cricket by our captain.

Ian 'Guy' Botham had been in for more than an hour, batting very responsibly, and at 134 for four we were still in with a chance of survival. The danger was the new ball, just five overs distant, and to hurry us towards the precipice Clive Lloyd had brought on Viv Richards and Larry Gomes to get through a few swift overs of off-spin. I am sure even he did not expect the free gift that Guy presented him with when he suddenly gave the charge to Viv, had visions of planting the ball firmly over the pavilion, and instead put it tamely into Holding's hands at long-off. Viv, one of Ian's closest friends, performed an impromptu dance of celebration while he wandered off, head hung low. He knew what he had done: no one needed to tell him when he came in. But I did wonder what was going through Fiery's mind. He had spent five hours out there for a patient 70 and he was out soon afterwards as Holding brought one up sharply under his chin. If Boycott's innings was the height of professionalism, Botham's shot was regrettably hot-headed, and the press inevitably crucified him for it.

Midway through the afternoon rain began to fall heavily, and it seemed that we might be saved by the elements after all. For some while – much too long, in my opinion – the umpires continued play, but finally the storm brought everyone off. As far as we were concerned it didn't last long enough. Tea was taken early and only another thirty-five minutes were lost to add to the twenty minutes at the start of the day when the ground staff appeared simply to have got behind with their preparations.

Peter Willey and Paul Downton sparked a final flicker of hope with another hour of defiance, but once one of them went the tail predictably perished instantly, to a ball still fairly new and an attack still fairly fresh. There could be no excuses. We always knew that we needed to play to our full potential to have a chance in this series, and in the opening round we had failed dismally. However good the attack – and this one must compare with the best there has ever been – no England side should be bowled out twice for less than 170.

Looking back, we left them too long to get at us. Perhaps we had attacked too much in the field, instead of making them work for every run, as we had done during our best period of the match on Saturday. If they were going to score 400-plus, we needed to leave ourselves less than three days to bat out. Port of Spain, it had been predicted, would present out best chance of a victory if the ball turned. Well, it didn't – not enough, anyway – but their bowlers performed superbly to drag the maximum help from a pitch which gave them only a little uneven bounce. It was depressing and deflating. The spirit of the side had taken an undoubted knock . . . and within twenty-four hours it was to take another.

3

Paradise Lost

Bob Willis went home on Friday, 20 February, and England were summarily robbed of a vice-captain, a character and one of only two genuine pace bowlers on the trip. To make matters worse the team were flying the same day to Guyana, where cricket riots were born and where street violence is part of folklore. They went there with spirits drooping and arrived to find that rain had been falling steadily for three days. In the endless tedium which followed, the personality of the touring party was put to its most severe test, and the results made fascinating viewing.

I had always liked Bob, but our friendship had grown much closer during the early weeks of this tour. He had confided in me a fair amount, both over his personal problems with the knee injury and over team affairs. I believe he knew that his knee problem was more serious than had originally been thought, and he prepared himself for the worst.

It happened on the morning after the end of the First Test. Nets were optional that day, and for reasons which I have mentioned earlier I was one of four or five players who did not attend. Bob was there, trying to bowl properly but knowing deep down that things were not right. He bowled no more than twenty deliveries before giving up in some pain and considerable despair. He was due to see a hospital surgeon again later that day, but I think he knew even then that he would be going home. The injury had been hanging around for almost three weeks by that stage. It was quite clearly not just a simple twist, and with two knee operations already behind him Bob knew only too well what complications could arise.

Contingency plans were being made by the management, with Bob's full support. When he returned from seeing the surgeon, whose opinion had been that the joint was unharmed but that the ligament might need surgery, the manager discussed the matter with him before reaching the unhappy but inevitable decision. Phone calls to England were made, a flight was booked, and without any doubt Bob felt helplessly choked. He is a wholehearted cricketer, totally committed to the England team and well liked and respected for it. He is also a humorous man of great character and intelligence. But above all he is sensitive, and I felt deeply for him that night.

Guy arranged a farewell party for Bob in his room, and although the free afternoon meant that players were scattered far and wide over the island most of the squad managed to get there during the evening. Graham Stevenson and Peter Willey performed a hilarious cabaret, at one point doing a sketch of Bob bowling in a wheelchair. Generally Bob was taking the whole sad affair very well, and hid his obvious concern at the fact that he would now once again be written off by some of the press. He had proved them wrong before, and I very much hoped he could do so again. A.C. (Alan Smith) had told most of us the bad news that evening, but as he could not get the entire party together the official announcement was delayed until the following morning, by which time it had already leaked into the British papers. I went to Bob's room soon after seven and we talked through many things, including his replacement, Robin Jackman.

Both of us were very pleased that Jackers had finally made it on to a tour, even if the circumstances were sad. Bob grew up with him in Surrey's second team, and I have played against him ever since I came into the Essex side. My first feeling, however, was that he would have a job to play much cricket. With the captain and Graham Dilley virtually assured of their Test places only one more seam bowler was needed, and it would take something remarkable for Robin to play ahead of either Chris Old or Graham Stevenson, both of whom had originally been selected ahead of him. I could not help thinking that we really did not need another seamer – how much more valuable it would have been to bring out an extra batsman. This was in no way derogatory to Jackers, whom I have always considered a fine bowler, but our experiences in Trinidad had convinced me that we were short of an experienced player to bat at three. Bob Woolmer or Dennis Amis would have been very useful. I know I was not alone in this opinion, but I could appreciate the management view that to recruit a batsman to replace a bowler would be showing very little confidence in the batters we already had with us. Mike Gatting and Roland Butcher were two who might feel they were being unfairly treated by such a move, as they had not even played in Trinidad.

So the decision was Jackers, and we were told that he would be with us inside three days. He had been an unlucky bowler throughout his career, regularly taking 70 or 80 wickets a year but often being overlooked for honours, to the benefit of lesser performers. Although he was thirty-five, his action has remained good and there seemed no doubt about his fitness. Some cricketers dislike Robin's antics on the field, where his appeals are quite unique, but I consider him very good value as an off-field character and potentially an ideal addition to a touring party.

He could hardly have chosen a worse spot to start. Guyana, we had all been warned, would be more of a sentence than a stay. Even nine years earlier, when I first went there with England Young Cricketers, reports had reached us of muggings in broad daylight, and everyone I talked to said that things were very much worse now. Before we set off the manager called us all together and laid down a set of rules for our fortnight in Georgetown. No one was to leave the hotel at night. During daylight hours, never go out in groups of less than three or four. Don't wear jewellery or watches in the streets. If we got the impression that we were in for a two-week confinement not unlike a prison camp, we were not disappointed. It might not have been so bad, but for the fact that we arrived in teeming rain and the weather did not improve for four days.

We descended through thick cloud into Georgetown, passing over immense, uninhabitable areas of jungle and swamp – the interior, they call it, but it looked to us very much like the end of the world. The locals greeted us with enthusiasm, but they told us enough about their recent weather to confirm that we would play no cricket for two or three days at least. On this tour, it was nothing new . . . but that didn't make it any better. The customary hour or so was spent, sardine-like, in the airport VIP lounge. A bus collected us for the fifty-minute drive into the city, past hundreds of wooden dwellings built on stilts to keep out snakes and lizards, and through poverty-stricken shanty towns. The Pegasus Hotel was a haven, far better than most of us expected, with small but functional rooms and views over the sea and the amazing wall, first built by the Dutch, which runs the length of the coastline to keep the ocean at bay.

Sadly, the curiosity of being below sea level was a distinct disadvantage when it came to cricket, for the drainage system at the Bourda ground consists of open gullies around the boundary fence. The gullies, we discovered, were full to bursting point and the outfield was like a lake. We could not play cricket. We could not go out. There was nothing left but to make ourselves as content as possible for what could be a lengthy stay in the hotel. Their English manager was very willing to help, and the room I shared with Peter Willey was quickly kitted out with a fridge, where we stored the Chablis we had brought in from Trinidad. Our respective tape players were rigged up, and even postcards were bought and written.

The extent of team activity on Saturday and Sunday was a morning session at a local indoor sports hall. We played three- and five-a-side football, which at least got everyone moving; but after two mornings in that steamy hall, where the mosquitoes bit you hungrily if you stood still long enough, everyone was becoming irritable and the programme needed altering. Evenings were spent in the team room which, unusually, was at lobby level and was more frequently used as a conference hall. In a place like Georgetown the team room becomes even more vital than usual, and the customary drinks, papers and card games were augmented by two extra entertainments. There was a racing game, played with three packs of cards, which caused a great deal of merriment and a fair amount of money changed hands. And, because Guyana has no television, there was a nightly film show by courtesy of the hotel's video equipment. On night two it was *Papillon*, particularly apt as it was filmed very close to Guyana, and we had our own live mosquitoes to match those in evidence on the screen.

One significant event occurred amid the monotony. Geoff Miller was appointed vice-captain in place of Bob Willis, after a vote among the seven men who originally picked the tour party the previous September. Three of them – the captain, manager and assistant manager – were with us on tour, and the remaining four were thousands of miles away back in England. Whether they considered Boycott among the candidates I don't know, but ironically he was in bed with a throat infection when the rest of the side were informed of the verdict. No one raised any objections, because Dusty is an experienced and well-liked cricketer, but it struck me immediately that a delicate situation could arise since he and Peter Willey would probably be contesting one position in the next Test. What none of us knew at that stage was that political interference of a totally unexpected nature was about to render all speculations on the coming Test redundant.

Certainly Robin Jackman had no idea of his unenviable role in the commotion to come as he landed in Guyana shortly after three in the morning on Monday, 23 February, after a journey of fits and starts which had taken him twenty-two hours door to door. The manager and Chris Old, who was to be Jackers' first roomie, met him at the airport and Robin sensibly opted to stay up for as long as

possible. He came down to breakfast looking conspicuously pale and tired, took the inevitable ribbings and then
joined us in our first practice session in Guyana. He must
have wondered just what he was letting himself in for. The
venue for the practice was a tennis court or, to be more
precise, two tennis courts. They belonged to a school and
stood by the side of a road – just two hard courts with a
makeshift net rigged up at the back of them. It was the first
time I had ever faced England's opening bowler rushing
in from the baseline on a school hard court, and the
experiment was no great success. Several balls were struck
across the road and lost, twelve more were ruined forever
by the surface of the court, and the whole thing was rather
a sad joke as a net facility for England's touring team. The
best that we could say about it was that it got us moving
after four days of doing virtually nothing.

I played tennis that afternoon and the following morning, and began to feel that I was in better form at that
game than I was at cricket! Matters were temporarily
improved when, after a great deal of hunting around the
city, Ken Barrington discovered a club ground above sea
level, perfectly dry and available to us. Ironically it was
less than half a mile from our hotel and belonged to the
state police, but it served a purpose and on the Tuesday
afternoon we were able to have a satisfactory middle
practice there.

Brian Rose took no part in that practice, and was to take
no further part in the tour. During the afternoon he visited
an eye specialist on the advice of Bernard Thomas, who
thought there might be something wrong with his eyesight
after watching him misjudge a catch in the deep at
Trinidad. Rather than make a fuss then, with a Test
match imminent, he waited until we reached Guyana, but
continued to watch Rosey carefully. He noticed that he
was reluctant to play tennis or squash, which is unusual
for him, and wondered whether that also might be connected. The specialist confirmed our fears. Rosey
returned to say that there was a defect in his right eye, and
we all silently assumed the worst from that moment on. It

seemed that we would be losing our second experienced player inside a week.

We were told officially later that evening, although nothing had at that stage been decided finally. The following afternoon Rosey went to see another specialist, who rubber-stamped the opinions of the first, and with no alternatives he realized he would have to go home. It had been a short and unhappy second tour for Brian Rose. From the moment that he was out to the third delivery of the opening game at Point-à-Pierre precious little went right for him. Essentially he is a quiet and reserved character and on this trip he was noticeably a loner, although by no means the only one in our squad. Naturally he was very distressed at the news, not just because he was missing the rest of the tour but because he knew that his future, just like Bob Willis' a week earlier, would now be questioned unless the London specialist he was to see next could come up with some remedy.

We thought we had suffered our share of misfortune and disturbance already, but within twenty-four hours the loss of another player seemed a minor handicap as we were thrust into a political row with far-reaching implications. The scenario could not have been more apt, for on the Tuesday evening the team was asked to attend a reception thrown by Roy Fredericks, the former West Indies and Glamorgan opener, now holding the title of 'Comrade' as Guyana's Minister for Sport. He had been in the job only a matter of weeks and I doubt if he relished what was about to happen any more than we did. Our attendance was compulsory because, we were led to believe, 'Comrade' Forbes Burnham, President of the Republic, was to be present. But he failed to turn up, so we stood around in groups for two hours, enlivened rather chillingly by witnessing a mugging on the street below the fourth-floor balcony where we were standing.

We had expected to be back in competitive action the following day, when a one-day game had been arranged against Guyana following the completely abortive four-day affair. However an early-morning inspection by Ken

Barrington found that the outfield was still far too muddy
for play. Looking back now, that would have been my last
chance of setting foot on the Test ground at Bourda. I left
Guyana without even seeing it.

The police ground was again made available to us, and
sides were chosen for a full-scale practice match amongst
ourselves, with a few local players making up the numbers. The team were arranged so that our first three or
four batsmen were facing our opening bowlers, so giving
both factions the best practice opportunities. I scored
50-odd, soured by a brief incident with Graham Dilley.
He bowled me a hostile bouncer, a very good delivery in
fact, which I fended off my head. The ball looped up off
my glove, and I momentarily lost my cool and swung my
left foot at it as it landed. I don't know whether it was a
result of my training with West Ham, but I caught the ball
perfectly on the half-volley and drove it straight towards
Picca's face as he followed through. Not surprisingly, he
was put out. He rushed in fiercely for the next couple of
balls, and a few words were exchanged between us. Later I
went to talk to him. Any animosity between us had long
gone, but he was still upset because, he said, too many
people on the tour were taking the mickey out of him. I
have said before that Graham is temperamental; he is also
sensitive and, being the youngest member of the squad, he
was finding it hard to come to terms with all the jokes at
his expense. He saw in them something malicious which
was never intended, and reacted by becoming more
moody and introverted. I tried to tell him that it had
happened in every side I had ever played for, and the only
way to handle it was to give some back himself.

That evening Alan Smith called us together and broke
the news that government inquiries were being made into
Robin Jackman's links with South Africa. It was common
knowledge among cricketers that Jackers had spent most
of his recent winters there, playing and coaching. His wife,
too, was South African. Nobody saw it as unusual,
because many English cricketers spend time there, so
this news came as a surprise and a puzzle. Personally,

however, I had no idea of the implications. Most of the squad had been to South Africa at one time or another. Five years earlier David Gower and Paul Downton had even been banned from entering Guyana because they had played there. Surely, most of us assumed, this was a storm in a teacup, some sort of administrative error which would be sorted out. Jackers did not seem very worried at that stage, and we all got down to talking about the one-day international scheduled for the following day.

It very nearly did not take place. When we met in the hotel lobby at 6.30 a.m., prepared for the unusual journey down the coast by military aircraft, most of the press contingent were milling around and something was clearly wrong. A report on Guyana's state radio station had said that Jackers would not be allowed to play cricket in the country. The manager, who had been summoned to the lobby an hour earlier by journalists bearing this news, had failed to get it confirmed. If it had been, we would not have gone to Berbice. My own feelings were strengthening by the minute. If this report was true, and Robin Jackman was banned from playing in Guyana, then I believed strongly that we should not play at all. He had been selected on the same basis as the rest of us; he was one of us, and if Guyana could not accept that they should not have any of us.

The Berbice match went on after a swift conference between A.C., Ken Barrington, Ian Botham and Geoff Miller. They probably felt they could not act on unconfirmed reports, and in any case Jackers had not been included in the side for this game, so there was no question of him being prevented from playing. Alan Smith stayed behind for what was to be a momentous day of talks. We had all been told to say nothing about the issue, and none of us was in any doubt now about the seriousness of the position. We travelled from the hotel to the military airstrip in a bus with the West Indies players. The Jackman affair was not discussed and I don't know what their team thought of it all. One aircraft and two helicopters had been provided for us by the Guyana Defence Force, which seemed ironic in the circumstances. We took the light aircraft while the West Indians went in the helicopters, and it was the least conventional journey to a match I have ever made. We landed on a strip of red dirt no more than 200 yards long, and were then lifted by helicopter on to the ground itself. Some of us were reminded of the television series *MASH*, in which wounded servicemen are laid on stretchers and strapped to the rubbers of helicopters to be lifted out of the camp. One mischievous suggestion was that it might be a useful method if Roberts or Holding were in particularly violent form! The entire journey had taken us only half an hour and we arrived in greater comfort than the press corps, most of whom had to travel the eighty miles by road, and take a ferry boat across the Berbice river. That method, which can take up to five hours if you have ferry problems, was one which I had experienced – we did the journey that way when I played for England Young Cricketers at Berbice in 1972. This second journey was far more satisfactory, but my abiding memory of my first trip in a helicopter is the ear-shattering noise.

We had a lot on our minds that day. It would have been difficult enough facing the West Indies in a one-day match as our first cricket in eight days, but in addition the rumblings over Robin Jackman in the background, and the knowledge that the entire tour was now at stake, did nothing for our confidence or spirit. An hour before the start came another scare. Geoff Boycott reported to the captain that he had a strained groin. I don't know what passed between them, but Geoff did eventually play. If he had not, the situation could have been intriguing. Peter Willey would presumably have opened with me, and it may have been felt that an extra seam bowler would be more useful than a spinner like Geoff Miller. The choice could just have been Robin Jackman!

We lost the toss and were put in to bat on a pitch which had a few damp spots. Boycott and I began well, but I was out playing a hook at Andy Roberts. It was a deliberate gambit of mine to try the hook in limited-overs situations,

49

because I saw it as one of the few shots that could regularly be played against their quick men with a fair chance of bringing runs. The half-volley, or simply the full-length ball of driving length, is a collector's piece, so I decided that when they bounced me I would go for it. The ball clipped my glove, and I was gone.

Significantly or otherwise, they brought on the change bowlers as soon as I was out. We had discussed them the previous night at our team meeting, concluding that the Mickey Mouse, as we called the fifth bowler, had to be punished if we were to have a realistic chance of a decent score. The plan went slightly haywire as Mickey, in the combined form of Larry Gomes and Viv Richards, took four wickets. Both managed to turn the ball and they ended up bowling their full quota of 10 overs each. Ian Botham and Peter Willey pulled us out of the mire a little before lunch, and even managed to get after Joel Garner for the first time on the tour, but we still managed only 136. Frankly it was not enough, and to have any chance we needed three or four wickets almost immediately.

Hopes were lifted when we picked up two – a prize pair, in fact. Gordon Greenidge was run out and Viv, tempted by Picca to hook despite the presence of two men back behind square, was well caught by Graham Stevenson. They were 11 for two and we were still in the game. Perhaps the turning point came two runs later. We were all convinced that Desmond Haynes was run out, but the umpire said not. He survived, played the only substantial innings of the game, and steered them to victory. Such is cricket.

Graham Dilley had been hit on the toe by Joel Garner while batting, and after two attempts to bowl he had to go off, leaving us very stretched. John Emburey bowled as well as ever, but the damp spots had dried and the ball no longer turned. He did succeed in bowling Everton Mattis, who had scored 24, and the dismissal caused an incident which in Mattis' home island of Jamaica could easily have been the prelude to a riot. For some odd reason Mattis declined to walk after the ball had hit leg-stump, clearly

suggesting that David Bairstow had knocked off the bails
with his pads. Most of us had heard the unmistakable
noise of ball against stump, quite apart from seeing it, but
several seconds of indecision by the umpires, and a quite
unnecessary conference, only exacerbated the situation.
Mattis, finally given out, went off looking upset and followed by a few harsh words from our closer fielders who,
quite understandably, felt that if you can't get them out
bowled, how can you?

The West Indians eventually beat us by six wickets,
which was no real surprise. We had known the previous
night that we needed to play at 100 per cent of our potential to have any real hope, and we simply didn't do it.
Thoughts turned rapidly back to the Jackman issue and
we did not have to wait long for developments – the time it
took a helicopter to fly us back to Georgetown, in fact. We
were put down on the army airfield, and a bus carried us
down the road 400 yards to the hotel. The scene which
awaited us suggested that the Queen was about to make a
visit. Television units from BBC and ITN were set up on
the steps of the hotel, various other cameramen were
poised to take pictures, and the journalists who had not
made the trip to Berbice were queuing up behind. I happened to be sitting next to Jackers, and as we got off the
bus together the cameras began to roll. We were hustled
through and upstairs to the captain's room, where we had
to wait two hours for Alan Smith to return from the High
Commission. Ian spoke to him on the phone and discovered the up-to-date position, which was even worse
than we had supposed. Jackers was not only to be banned
from playing, but was to be deported.

It meant, inevitably, that the Second Test would be
cancelled, for there was no possibility that the England
cricket authorities would allow one member of the squad
to be deported while the others stayed to play. It also
meant that we would all be leaving Guyana as quickly as
practicable, and after the depressing week we had been
through nobody was the slightest bit upset, except Jackers. He had spoken to his wife on the phone and she had

51

told him that photographers and journalists had been knocking on their front door. Plainly he was worried about her, and quite understandably. All of us felt very sorry for him, too, having waited so long for his first tour and now thrust into a political row without even playing a game. Alan Smith returned to tell us the news officially, bringing with him a statement from the Cricket Council leaving no one in any doubt that England would not be dictated to on selection issues. We were told that we were heading for Barbados, and that we should be ready to leave at one hour's notice.

At this stage no one knew whether the tour could continue in any form. We speculated among ourselves on the possibility that we might soon be heading home, and that England might never again make a full tour of the Caribbean. It was a strange evening: discussions were taking place in groups scattered all around the hotel, pressmen were racing hither and thither, and no player quite knew his future beyond the next few hours. Any thoughts of a replacement for Brian Rose were swept on one side, for all we knew never to be revived. Cricket became very much a background issue as the politicians took over, and we felt that we were just the innocent footballs which could be kicked from one end of the Caribbean to the other. Graham Dilley added another touch of irony. He feared that the big toe on his right foot might in fact be broken. Certainly it was too badly injured for him to play for a few days, and with Chris Old still suffering from a trapped nerve in his shoulder Jackers would almost certainly have been in our side for the phantom Second Test!

4

Mixed Blessings

The tour was now in turmoil. What is more, the future direction of world cricket was suddenly under threat from the type of political situation which has become nauseatingly common in recent years. Racial matters were again interfering with a sport famous for its unquestioning acceptance of all races and all colours. The anomaly was cruelly ironic, and just one more thing for England's players to ponder in the next few fraught hours. Not that they had long to wait. A flight out of Guyana was arranged for them on Friday, 27 February, and at the hour when under normal circumstances they would have been sitting down to their eve-of-Test team dinner the players were being warmly welcomed to Barbados with the customary rum punch and steel band.

For four more days uncertainty ruled every action. The Jackman affair had transgressed far beyond the powers of cricket administrators. Whether England stayed in the Caribbean or flew home, probably never to return, depended on the leading politicians of the West Indian islands. They took their time making the decision and chose their moment with an eccentric regard for melodrama. It was 1 a.m. on Wednesday, 4 March when the smiling figure of Henry Forde, Foreign Affairs Minister of the Barbados government, emerged at the door of villa number 213 at the Rockley Resort complex, four miles outside Bridgetown. Television cameras clicked and whirred into action, eight diligently persistent journalists pressed forward to record what might have been a devastating moment for international sport, and Mr Forde, bonhomie personified, distributed copies of a three-page statement compiled by the governments of Antigua, Barbados, Jamaica and Montserrat — England's four remaining stops on the tour.

Squinting through the gloom, while deafened by the background symphonies of crickets and frogs, not to mention the erotic splashings and squeals of a group of nude bathers in a neighbouring pool, it was still possible to ascertain that the statement dealt almost exclusively with Caribbean abhorrence of apartheid. It got to the point at the foot of page two, in a single paragraph which resolved the doubts and fears of a week no one involved would easily forget. It read as follows:

> The present case, raising as it does the third party principle, must therefore be treated on its own merits. In view of this, and after the most careful and searching consideration and having regard to all the circumstances involved, the Governments of Antigua, Barbados, Jamaica and Monserrat have jointly concluded that the remainder of the cricket tour should be permitted to continue as scheduled.

Radio Barbados broke the news to me when I woke up on the Wednesday morning. As usual I switched on the hotel's radio system, and the tour verdict was among the first items on the news. It may sound a strange way for an England player to be told of his immediate future, but it was symptomatic of a row which had got completely out of hand.

My first feelings were of confusion: I simply wasn't sure whether to be pleased or not. Throughout the preceding week we had all been in this strange limbo, and the endless questions and doubts had bred an unhealthy atmosphere. Frankly, I believe a lot of the boys had taken all they could swallow. If it had been cancelled forthwith there would have been no tears, but the odd smile might easily have broken through – something which had been unusually rare in recent days. All kinds of fringe worries had clouded everyone's thoughts. Paramount among them was the knowledge that most of our wives were due to join us in Barbados, and the panic phone calls crossing the Atlantic were the norm rather than the exception. Brenda phoned me more than once, wanting to know what would happen if the tour was abandoned. She said she had never watched and listened to so many news broadcasts, and felt that most people believed we would soon be on our way home.

It was impossible to practise with proper enthusiasm, or to apply adequate forward thinking to the matches to come, when we were well aware that the next plane leaving for Heathrow could be ours. Every morning we picked up the two Barbados morning papers to read the latest speculation on the political thinking, and the latest whims and beliefs of the apparently never-ending stream of leader writers these two papers could conjure up. Some of the comment pieces were close to vitriolic, certainly misguided, and our feeling of helplessness increased by the hour.

We had all been delighted, not to mention relieved, to get out of Guyana, where the overwhelming emotion had been one of opposition, from politicians if not from the public, to our very presence there. Arriving in Barbados after a two-hour delay at Georgetown airport and a flight on an aircraft with no air conditioning was like arriving in a political haven. We were met on the tarmac by officials of the island cricket association – not in itself unusual, but this time they were noticeably anxious to please. Drinks waiters swarmed around us in the newly built arrivals lounge, and although there was no escape from the television crews or radio microphones, everybody raised their spirits several degrees within minutes of arriving. Jackers himself looked measurably more relaxed. On the flight from Guyana he had sat on the inside of Alan Smith, the manager looking like a protector. Yet both were so exhausted by recent events that they slept through the flight.

With minimal delay we were taken to the Holiday Inn, which is just how it sounds. After the oppression of Guyana we were able to sit in the restaurant built on a jetty next to the beach and look out on a scene out of a holiday brochure. This, I thought, was the Caribbean as everyone at home imagined it to be, and it could have been a million miles removed from Guyana. Most of us had visited Barbados before, on holidays or private tours if not with England, and the days which followed were quite unlike any part of an international cricket series. It was not that we tried to forget cricket – we practised daily, kept fit and simulated match conditions between ourselves. In between we indulged in tennis, water skiing or horse riding. It probably sounds very relaxing, yet none of us could feel content.

It had not been a happy tour, even before this business; it was simply unpleasant. I believe if a vote had been taken during those few days most of the team would have chosen to go home, and very few would have been concerned about future visits to the West Indies. By reading the papers we learned that a decision was likely to be made on the Tuesday. Foreign ministers of the four relevant countries were, we understood, to meet in Barbados. Although I did not know it at the time, it transpired that they had to reach a vote of unanimous approval or the tour would have to be abandoned. On that particular day our practice programme – devised by an increasingly frustrated management team – comprised a full-scale match within the squad, with teams led by Ian Botham and Geoff Miller, just as we had played in Georgetown on the day that the Jackman affair was born. I happened to spend all that day on the field in blistering heat, batting through our team's innings for a century, and when I returned to the Holiday Inn I felt drained. An unusual sight met us – about twenty-five British journalists were camped around one table in the hotel lobby, on top of which lay a phone. That number had been given to the government offices and a call was promised immediately a statement was available.

I learned later that most of the journalists sat by that phone from four in the afternoon until around eleven at night, at which point some enterprising soul discovered that the ministers had reconvened four miles away at Rockley Resort. Those who had not given up and retired to bed made the midnight trek to Rockley, a straggling village of villas with a golf course threading through it, and they were rewarded with a verdict in bizarre surroundings at dead of night. Whatever the individual reaction to the 'yes' vote, it was a load off our collective shoulders. The uncertainty had put us under the greatest pressure. Morale had slid to a low ebb, as I am certain it would have done within any group of men in similar circumstances.

Now at least we knew where we stood. We knew, too, that our wives could enjoy their holidays with us. Alan Smith said that we would probably have been allowed to stay on in Barbados for a fortnight or so if the tour had been called off, although officially we remained under contract to the TCCB (Test and County Cricket Board) until April and, if they had so wished, they could have arranged a substitute series, perhaps in India or Pakistan. Alan Smith called a team meeting during the day to clear the air, and we all knew we were back in cricket business when Fiery, with some indignation, raised the subject of inadequate net facilities. Twenty-four hours earlier such a discussion would have seemed pointless, but now we had to restore our brains to cricket thinking. It was not going to be easy. For me it began with an unexpected row which brought into the open the minor frustrations that had been welling up inside me for weeks past.

I attributed my exhaustion the previous evening to having been on the field the whole day in blistering heat. That night, in a local pub, I had been close to falling asleep, and among the people with me was Ian Botham. At the meeting Ian raised the subject of players running before breakfast, saying he thought it was a bad thing in the Caribbean climate and that it should be banned. He cited me as an example, and suggested that I would not have been so tired the previous night if I hadn't gone for my usual morning run. I disagreed, because I believed the running was doing me good. From there the discussion broadened to touch on a number of other tour matters, and for a few minutes Ian and I exchanged some fairly strong views. It was, in many ways, a healthy argument at a difficult time on a tour. Within a few hours it was forgotten and we were back on good terms; neither of us is the type to bear grudges.

The mundane matters of any tour once more came to the forefront. We had asked for an increase in our meal allowances for as long as we were in Barbados, since most of us found that 20 dollars for lunch (about £4.50) and 50 dollars for dinner was not enough to meet the high tourist prices. In another way, however, that meeting was a worrying one, because so little was said about the important things. Team spirit had taken a battering, and it was going to be very difficult to motivate ourselves for the remainder of the series. Yet these things, whether deliberately or accidentally, were taking a back seat.

A large contingent of players' wives arrived the following day, including Brenda. I am well aware that some people involved in the game view this day with trepidation, seeing it as potentially divisive. To me it provides a welcome reunion for both parties, and in most cases the team members play at least as well, if not better.

A day later the airport arrivals included one C. W. J. Athey. Normally a replacement player receives a fanfare of publicity on tour, so it was a commentary on our unusually newsworthy situation that Bill slipped into the country almost unnoticed. Everyone had been so concerned with political ramifications in recent days that the matter of a new player had inevitably become a low priority. It seemed an eternity since Brian Rose had flown out of Guyana. Athey had come from Australia, where had had been playing grade cricket, via such romantic spots as Hawaii and Pago-Pago. The journey had taken him twenty-two hours and, although he was at the Holiday Inn by mid-afternoon on the Friday, the selectors considered it would be unfair to ask him to play in the four-day game against Barbados starting the following morning. They were probably right, but it unfortunately meant that he was also a non-starter for the Third Test a week later, which cut our options considerably.

Like Robin Jackman, Bill was among the five official standby players, who were paid by the TCCB to keep themselves fit and available for just such an emergency. So naturally no one was surprised that he was chosen for the job. He is regarded as one of England's leading batting prospects, and the policy of playing three or four players of twenty-three or twenty-four, all expected to improve, has obvious merits. In this instance, however, I believe Bill Athey was the wrong choice. I have nothing whatever against him as a person or as a cricketer, but I was concerned at the acute shortage of experience in our squad, heightened by the loss of two senior players in Rose and Bob Willis. Asked for my opinion, I said that Bob Woolmer, the accomplished opener from Kent, should have been the man recruited. Not only could he have filled the problematical number three role very adequately, but he would also have been a very competent stand-in if anything had happened to Geoff Boycott or myself.

In seventeen days since the Trinidad Test ended, our match action had been confined to two one-day games. We could scarcely have selected more formidable opponents with which to resume our first-class programme, for Barbados could put out five fast bowlers of Test calibre in Joel Garner, Wayne Daniel, Malcolm Marshall, Sylvester Clarke and Hartley Alleyne. It seemed to us that they must have a pace-bowling factory in Bridgetown. Everywhere you looked – on the beaches, in the streets and in the parks – small boys were imitating their favourite bowler, racing in to hurl it down as fast as they could. It struck me that this was part of the reason for our own shortage of quick bowlers in recent years – it was an ongoing situation, difficult to arrest, because British kids have no one to emulate. Neither Garner nor Alleyne was in the side against us, but the trio which remained were a fearsome enough combination. As support they could call on former Test off-spinner Albert Padmore, and all-rounder Collis King, whose batting had won the West Indies the World Cup Final in 1979. The opening batsmen were Gordon Greenidge and Desmond Haynes, and wicketkeeper David Murray completed their remarkable quota of Test players which made them possibly the strongest first-class team in the world.

One of my priorities on the opening morning was to

study the wicket and consult the groundsman over his plans for the Test. He informed me, to my undisguised alarm, that he intended to leave a good covering of grass on the pitch. I asked him, half humorously, if that was because he wanted the match finished inside three days, and his deadpan answer was that the wicket would hold together longer that way. All it did for me was confirm the suspicion that the opening session or two of the Test could could be a very lively experience, and that we would almost certainly be well advised to bowl first, given the luck of the toss. In the island game that day, however, Ian Botham called wrongly, and to no one's surprise we were put in to bat.

I was first out for 26, pushing unconvincingly half-forward to Clarke and dragging the ball into my stumps from outside-off. Back in the dressing-room, irritated with myself, the classic line came into mind – I had been bowled by a ball I should have left alone! The match was destined to be drawn once it had taken us a day and a half to accumulate 298. Boycott, Botham, Butcher and Willey all made runs and got in much-needed practice at occupying the crease, but in terms of competitive entertainment it was a non-event. Not that too many people were there to show their annoyance – we had long ago learned that the West Indian public is reluctant to turn up for anything but international cricket, an attitude which kills a few myths about their fanaticism for the game.

Barbados, in fact, achieved a first-innings lead of 36, but after a typically hurricane start through Greenidge and Haynes they were barely faster than we had been. John Emburey again bowled with superb control, taking five wickets in a spell very reminiscent of his Trinidad Test performance. But perhaps more notable were the four wickets taken by Robin Jackman in his first bowl on tour. After all that he had been through, we naturally wondered just how Jackers would react when he was finally able to play some cricket. The answer was quick and comforting. He bowled straight, making the batsmen play at everything, and showing all the virtues of economy and accuracy for which he is renowned in county cricket. If the rest of the game was in itself meaningless, that spell had been enough to influence our selection for the Third Test. Chris Old was dropped, and Robin Jackman, only just emerged from a political nightmare, was to realize his lifetime dream at last.

5

Tears for a Friend

England were beaten as comprehensively in the Third Test as they had been in the First – the margin an arguably less humiliating 298 runs. The Kensington Oval ground in Bridgetown echoed to its customary heady sounds of calypso beat and Caribbean celebrations, this time augmented by two thousand Britons, over specially for the Test and conspicuous by their pale pink skins and their garb which, in many misguided cases, looked like a Monty Python-style parody of South Pacific. *Gooch and Viv Richards made centuries, just as they did at Lord's in 1980. Clive Lloyd made one too, perhaps the decisive innings on the opening day.*

But although the cricket was attractive and the atmosphere diverting, the occasion will be remembered with sadness long after the result and details are forgotten statistics. Ken Barrington, one of the finest, friendliest men cricket has ever known, died of a massive heart attack on the night of Saturday, 14 March. The effect on the players, who adored and respected him, was unimaginably devastating.

Brenda had decided to join me on my morning runs, and on that awful Sunday we had been back in the room only a few minutes when, at 7.30, there was a knock on the door. I answered it to find Alan Smith and Ian Botham on the threshold, in itself enough to tell me that something was wrong. Alan said he had some bad news and the first thing that entered my head was that someone was dead. I don't know why I thought that, even now, but perhaps it was a naturally pessimistic reaction at a time when the tour seemed fated to suffer endless disasters.

This one, however, was different. When they told me Kenny had died I refused to take it in. I stood dumbly for a moment, then muttered that I couldn't believe it. Not Kenny. Not now. Captain and manager left me, to continued their dreadfully reluctant tour of the players' rooms. I did not envy them that: I just had to come to terms with the fact that I had lost a man who meant more to me than almost anyone in cricket. I also had to tell Brenda. She had been in the shower when I was told, and I knew how badly she would take it. If there was one person who always made her feel welcome, on a tour or at home, and who would go out of his way to organize things for all the wives, it was dear old Kenny. Brenda burst into tears, and my resistance snapped too: I broke down and cried.

A team meeting had been called for eight o'clock. The manager's room was a suite at the end of the pier, adjoining a disused night club which we used for get-togethers. Mostly they are happy affairs, full of fun or, at their most serious, full of determined talk about cricket. That Sunday there was no fun, no laughter . . . just solemn faces, visible emotion and tears. Alan Smith spoke to us briefly as a group – not that there was anything he could say to soften the blow. Then Bernard Thomas gave a medical explanation of what had happened. After that, the entire squad stood in silence for a minute to remember a man who was very much more than one of the management team.

Nothing was too much trouble for Kenny, and he once said that if he thought it would make us a better team he would wash all our socks for us. He had never wanted to give up playing (ironically, his first heart attack came only months after his retirement), but he saw that involvement with the side, both as a selector and a manager, was the next best thing. He revelled in the daily routine of a tour. The day before he died we had been talking together, and he told me he had been on twenty-six tours – and would do another twenty-six if he could.

I have already mentioned that he was hilariously

63

gullible. He also had a habit of confusing words, and during this tour he had got himself mixed up when trying to order a drink called a *piña colada*. 'I'll have one of those Peter Granadas," he had said to the baffled waiter, adding the well-known Barrington chuckle and wide, toothy grin. This was typical Kenny, and he knew he would be mimicked for days. But he took all the mickey-taking in the right spirit and gave plenty back. Kenny often became flustered if the organization of matters such as nets and transport went wrong. He was a worrier, not just about the menial things but about the future of the England team. It caused him endless hours of anxiety, and perhaps the strain – which he so rarely showed publicly – was finally too much. His great value to the team was as a confidant, not only in technical matters but in every aspect of a tour. He was a father-figure and everybody who had made a tour under him grew to love him like one of their own family. I saw little of his own playing career at close quarters, but enough to appreciate that he was talented and extraordinarily brave. His left arm remained permanently crooked from the battering Charlie Griffith gave it.

He had helped me enormously in Australia on the two previous tours, where my technique had needed tightening up. But, still more important, he had played a major part in moulding my attitude to batting. 'When you get in, make it count,' he used to say, 'because you might be rolled over quickly in your next three knocks and then you'll be sorry you failed to turn 50 into a big 100.' It was sound advice – simple, maybe, but the type of thing that every young player needs drumming into his brain. I have since started repeating it to the youngsters at Essex. Kenny also improved my concentration, something he had never lacked as a batsman. There were times on earlier tours when he had been reticent about suggesting things to players in case they thought him presumptuous and interfering. But in the West Indies he had been given special responsibilities for such matters – and in any case he knew by then how much we all respected his judgement.

It is unusual for anyone a generation older than the team to command such a degree of respect. So many people try to tell us how to play, and many of them are well meaning but misinformed. A man like Ken Barrington, however, was a gem, because we all knew just how much cricket knowledge he had stored up in that curly-haired head. No words of mine can fully explain what he meant to the team. It is enough, perhaps, to describe the scene on that Sunday morning when we reached the ground for the third day of the Third Test. It had been decided that the match must go on, no matter how we felt; Kenny would have hated it any other way. We netted half-heartedly, trying wanly to make each other forget, knowing we never could. Then came the worst moment of all, as the teams lined up outside the pavilion and Peter Short, President of the Barbados Cricket Association, addressed the capacity crowd over the public address. His speech was brief but touching, and he called for a silent tribute.

The shock of it all got through to us then, and there were tears in everyone's eyes around me. Back in the dressing-room those of us who had been especially close to Kenny felt very miserable. Up in the press box some of the Fleet Street journalists who had known Kenny for years were wiping their eyes and blowing their noses. It was difficult to comprehend that we were in the middle of a Test match which had to continue, and I felt particularly bad because a split finger – suffered, ironically, when Kenny hit the ball to me during slip catching practice the previous day – was preventing me from fielding. No one felt like going out, but I was able to hide my sorrow in the dressing-room. Robin Jackman, a Surrey colleague of Ken's, was one of the worst affected. He had to bowl the opening over of the day, and I will always remember his words to me that lunchtime: 'I never thought I would be crying my eyes out as I ran in to bowl in my first Test match.'

The boys' performance that day was extremely professional in the circumstances, but by then it would have needed far more than professionalism to change the course of a Test we had been losing from the middle of the second day. England had crumbled to 72 for four, our top-order batting once more failing to cope with the best pace attack most of us will ever face, and the efforts of our bowlers in dismissing the West Indies for 265 looked likely to go unrewarded.

At first, everything had gone well for us. There were no illusions left in our thoughts and we knew, at the Test-eve dinner, that the opposition would have to play below par to give us a chance. We also badly needed to win that toss, and allow our seamers to exploit the help from the pitch, at the same time protecting our batsmen. So far, so good. We won the toss, put them in, and within nine overs they were 25 for two with Greenidge and Richards both gone. It was a dream start for Jackers, brought on as first change to bowl the eighth over and taking Greenidge's wicket with his fifth delivery. The ball moved enough off the pitch to defeat Gordon's defensive stroke, and he edged it at comfortable height to me at second slip.

Richards survived only one ball, then got a beauty from Picca. It flew high to the left of Ian Botham at second slip, but he plucked it out of the air to send his great friend on his way. We could barely believe such a start. Jackers continued to bowl accurately and well throughout his first spell in a Test, and at 47 he added the wicket of Haynes, who drove at a ball which left him slightly and was caught behind by Bairstow. I was delighted for Robin, because he had deserved a cap after all these years. Yet my feelings about him had not essentially altered from the time he arrived in Guyana. I had said then that I could not see him playing much cricket. The fact that he was in the side, and performing so capably, was a sad commentary on the disappointing form of Chris Old and Graham Stevenson, whom I had fancied to keep him out.

By lunch the West Indies were 72 for four, Mattis having fallen l.b.w. to Botham, but that was to be the peak of our achievements. Clive Lloyd was at the crease, and inside four hours he had dashed most of our hopes with a century made up of punishing strokes, after flailing his bat outside off-stump and connecting with devastating power. Larry Gomes kept him company, playing the supporting role he enjoys, and together they put on 154 for the fifth wicket – more than half the eventual total – and this was a critical factor in deciding the match.

We had struggled to contain them with only three seamers. The wicket still had some life, but our bowlers could not keep going without help and John Emburey had to come on in a purely defensive role, knowing that off-spin was unlikely to bowl out anyone on such a grassy first-day pitch. We rallied well in the final forty minutes, taking three more wickets. It should have been four, but I dropped Andy Roberts from the last ball of the day – a galling miss as we had already experienced his ability to slog any bowler off a length. It was, nevertheless, a satisfying start, a day on which we could all hold our heads high and when the hordes of supporters who had flown out from England could boast for once, instead of complaining. We still had to bat, though, and the thought hung over our heads like a wet towel. We had already conceded more than 200 runs – if we allowed them to approach 300, we were destined to struggle if their bowlers found there was still enough in the pitch to encourage them.

The tail-enders added a further 27 runs the next morning, which was not in itself a tragedy, but I was dismayed that Graham Dilley bowled with no hostility against players he should have dismissed with little difficulty. There was no need to bowl bouncers – he just had to run in at full pace and make them hurry. Ian had to take him off, and finally took all three wickets himself. Picca has all the basic requirements for a Test fast bowler and he is still very young, but he has a lot to learn.

Our reply could hardly have had a worse start. I scored six from Roberts' opening over, then stood at the non-striker's end while Michael Holding exploded into his fastest form from the first ball he delivered to Fiery. Five exceptionally quick balls, all just short of a length and rising, but none qualifying as bouncers, were negotiated with varying degrees of discomfort as the new ball bounced chest-high. The sixth was straight and of full length and knocked out the off-stump while Geoff tried to adjust, having initially looked to go on the back foot. Holding is an unusually athletic quick bowler, and has the ability to reach top pace without the over of looseners which such bowlers normally need. For the second over of a Test innings he was sensationally fast, and the Saturday crowd, packed in the stands, ringed around the boundary boards and balanced on corrugated iron roofs, bayed and chanted their approval.

It was no time for Mike Gatting to be coming in. This was his first try at number three in a Test, and he was virtually opening against Roberts and Holding at full throttle. He lasted less than an over before nicking Roberts to third slip, and we were 11 for two. I was playing with no great conviction, but in such a fraught start I needed some luck to survive. I had a break or two and began to feel good. David Gower and I had put on 29 when I chopped a ball into my stumps for the second time in a week on the Bridgetown ground. If I was irritated with myself the first time, I was really angry now. Other than being run out, or caught down the leg-side off the middle of the bat, there are no more frustrating methods of dismissal. Roland Butcher took my place, applauded all the way to the middle. It must have been a fantastic feeling for Butch on his native island, and I was relieved and gratified that the crowd had treated him so well, instead of seeing him as a defector as some feared they might.

The conditions were by now heaven-sent for the West Indian attack. Not only was the wicket one they would like to have packed up in their cricket trunks and carried around, but the sky was overcast for the first time in the match, aiding movement and keeping them cooler. The rain began at an awkward time, and Gower suffered for the second occasion in the series. Just as in Trinidad, the umpires conferred and decided to play on while he was batting. As soon as he was out – this time caught at slip off Croft – they called the players off. I have seen this occur in

England, so I am not blaming the individual umpires. But I do feel it is an unfair inconsistency which ought to be tightened up. The rain, to my eyes at least, was no heavier when they came off than when they had conferred earlier. The difference was that a wicket had been lost, and a precious one in our difficult position.

The delay was only twenty-five minutes but Butch did not last long afterwards before becoming another victim of Croft. Peter Willey came in and spent half an hour on nought, and he and the captain appeared to be arresting the slide when Holding returned for an over as spectacular as his first. He beat Ian Botham twice, and the second occasion produced a bad piece of cricket. Ian, obviously frustrated as another delivery took off past his chin from not very short, threw down his bat in clear agitation. It was not a protest against the bowling, just a gesture of helplessness – and as such it did nothing for the confidence of the low-order batsmen watching from the dressing-room with their pads on. No one likes the quick bowlers, and the tail-enders like them less than anyone. To see their captain, a highly regarded Test batsman, lay down his arms even in mock surrender is not heartening.

To make matters worse, Botham was dismissed by the fourth ball of the over, caught by a juggling David Murray. David Bairstow was out second ball and Holding was the local hero again. We were 94 for seven and there seemed no way out. Willey once more showed his fighting qualities, but steadily ran out of partners. Robin stayed with him for 15 overs, interrupted by the smoke from a nearby fire which actually sent the players off the field for several minutes, but we were all out for 122, twenty minutes before stumps; Willey was still there with 19 after batting valiantly for two hours.

I would not have backed many Test sides to make over 200 on that attack in such conditions, and our own total probably reflected the deficiencies that every one of us knew existed. Even the rapid loss of the tail is important. Against most other sides number nine, ten and eleven can often conjure up 50 runs between them, which can prove vital later in a match. Against these four bowlers we had no right to expect such bonuses. We were a little cheered when Dilley picked up Greenidge's wicket cheaply in the ten minutes remaining. As an opener, I can imagine the apprehensions in Gordon's mind during a period that no batsman wants to be burdened with. If you have to go out and start an innings any time in the last hour, it is always in the back of your mind that you must be there in the morning, so you tend to play unnaturally – and often you pay for it.

If we were still a little depressed when we filed off the ground that Saturday evening, it was nothing compared with the state of devastation the following morning. Kenny was dead, and for some while the match seemed scarcely to matter. In fact, as I have said, we performed creditably. Although Viv scored his first century of the series, he was never allowed to play with the freedom he craves, and the scoring rate was restricted to three an over throughout this most difficult of days. The West Indies finished it with a lead of 388, five wickets intact and Richards and Lloyd ominously still together. Following the rest day, which to most of us was part relief and part disaster as we had time to think about our situation, the worst happened and these two great batsmen added another 120 runs in the first hundred minutes.

To my mind, Lloyd went on too long. An hour before lunch on the fourth day he had a lead of 462. What point was there in prolonging the torture? Perhaps he feared a repeat of the occasion a few years ago when India scored 400-plus to beat them. If so, it was a fear tinged with fantasy, for we would have needed to score at more than 40 an hour, or almost four runs an over, and make more than twice as many as we had managed in any previous innings. As it transpired, the tactics were justified and we were well beaten anyway. Lloyd batted on until lunchtime, by which time he was out for 66 but Viv was unbeaten on 182 – a steady innings which became more spectacular through the morning as he appeared almost to select by numbers the balls he would destroy.

We were required to survive for ten hours or –
mathematically possible but logically ridiculous – score
523 to win. The odds against us were overwhelming but I
still saw a ray of hope. We needed a few breaks and a great
deal of determination, but I felt that if Fiery and I could
only get off to a start, on a wicket now much flatter and
easier than on earlier days, the others might take heart
and fight it through. All such optimism was demolished
within six minutes. Again the hatchet was in the hands of
Holding, and again Boycott failed to last his opening over.
This time it was the fifth ball, lifting again and taking the
edge before flying to Garner at gully. As if that was not a
bad enough blow, Mike Gatting was bowled by the next
delivery and we were two for two. Holding was mobbed at
fine leg by a fan club which had grown noticeably through
the game, and he certainly gave a fine performance. Many
critics have doubted his stamina and efficiency over the
years, but here was all too vivid proof that he still ranks as
the quickest in the world.

Our task now was virtually impossible, but David
Gower and I brought it back to the realms of reality with a
stand of 120 which took us well past tea and persuaded
Lloyd to resort to the off-spin of Richards – something he
would naturally have hoped to avoid. Viv is not the big-
gest spinner of a ball, but he performed very sensibly,
mixing up an over with three off-breaks and three seamers
swinging away from the bat. Good tactics, but no one
should have got out to him. However Lulu Gower played
a lazy shot, lacking concentration, and dragged the ball
into his off-stump. He had scored 54 and batted extremely
well, but he knew it was not enough. I had several times
gone up to him between overs and told him not to take
things too easily against Viv, but he fell into the trap.
Later that evening he found me and apologized, saying
how annoyed and upset with himself he was.

Losing one wicket to Richards would have been care-
less; losing two was much worse. Butch was the second
man out to him and Viv came off with two for 18 from 14
overs. Botham was out almost immediately to Roberts,

and although I was still there at the close on 88, I knew the rest would be academic. Croft, difficult enough to play anyway, had not helped our cause by going round the wicket for a spell and running straight on down the line of off-stump. Umpire Douglas Sang Hue administered one official warning and Croft went back to bowling over the wicket. But the damage was done, and this touch of gamesmanship had created a loose patch nicely on a length for anyone operating from the other end.

I completed my 100 the next morning and thought instantly of Kenny. He would have enjoyed it, I am sure, because he had worked so hard on my technique and application. Throughout the five hours it had taken me I had kept talking to myself, urging myself to keep concentrating. I deliberately forced my mind on to what Kenny had always told me – to make them count once you are established – and his words spurred me on. I still subconsciously expected him to be there when I got back to the dressing-room. The only consolation was that he inspired me to achieve that century.

It made no difference to the result. Peter Willey, who had stuck with me for 98 minutes, got an unlucky l.b.w. verdict against him, Bairstow was out second ball just as he had been in the first innings, and I followed quickly to a gully catch I could hardly believe. Joel Garner made it look almost easy, but I had struck it well and the ball had risen only inches off the ground. Croft was the man who finally twisted the knife with those three wickets in the space of five balls. John Emburey and Robin Jackman, not men to throw in the towel, pluckily kept them at bay for a while and took the game into the afternoon. But twenty minutes after lunch it was over. Despite my century, it was probably the saddest game I shall ever play in.

6

Heads above Water

The Fourth Test was saved by dint of three splendid English innings and a full day of rain. Just for a change, a Test passed off without major disruptions, personal or political, and England will remember Antigua considerably more fondly than most of the previous centres they had visited. But first they spent six days in Montserrat, the volcanic 'Emerald Isle' of the Caribbean, and this seemingly insignificant interlude was not without incident.

If you are looking for a holiday away from it all, as the travel brochures are fond of saying, Montserrat might well be your place. But in terms of accommodating an international cricket tour we discovered that this charming little island in the Antilles had limitations. Our problems began as soon as we arrived. The hotel into which the team were booked, standing on a hill overlooking the seaside ground, had only seventeen rooms, which meant there was not enough space for the group of wives who were still with us. A complicated arrangement by which certain players and their ladies were to move out to some villas broke down when it was discovered that the villas were four miles away. Finally, some alternative villas were found almost next door to the hotel. But after that game of musical rooms had been resolved, those of us left in the hotel had other things on our minds.

Our rooms were down a corridor which resembled the prison block in the television series *Porridge*. Doors slammed noisily, and the acoustics were such that you could hear a key turn two doors away. Our first night there was a

73

disaster, as there was no water, hot or cold, in the hotel. The following morning, although the supply had been restored, the lavatories were not operating, so I was up at 7 a.m. filling buckets of water from the shower and pouring them into the cistern. At breakfast, most of us being big eaters, we attempted to order egg, sausage and bacon, but were told that if you ordered egg you could only have sausage *or* bacon with it. You could also not have a large orange juice if you had coffee. The permutations kept us amused for some time, but they were another minor irritation. Someone then phoned the local car hire company to order one of their 'fleet' of vehicles for the day. 'I'm sorry,' came the reply. 'Our car is already out on order!' It would be churlish to complain loudly about such things in isolation, but, thrown together in a twenty-four-hour period, they at least illustrate that a cricket tour does not consist exclusively, of five-star VIP treatment.

Our one fixture in Montserrat was a four-day match against the Leeward Islands, an unremarkable occasion which even most of the locals chose to ignore. Despite being given a public holiday on the third day – the first two had fallen over a weekend anyway – the crowds were very small and no doubt disappointed the local cricket authorities. There are in any case only about 13,000 people on Montserrat, and there seemed little real fervour for the game. Their most popular citizen, however, is undoubtedly Jim Allen, the batsman who represented the West Indies in World Series cricket but has never won a Test cap. Allen was absent for our visit, having treatment in New York for an eye injury, and since Viv Richards and Andy Roberts, the two enduring stars of the Leewards side, were also missing, we were playing a depleted side with few names known to us.

We won – our first victory outside limited-overs matches since the opening game – but made hard work of a fourth-innings target of 174, losing five wickets for 109 before Butch came good, playing some typical shots in an unbeaten 77. I had been rested, along with David Gower, Peter Willey, John Emburey and Ian Botham, so the side was led by Geoff Miller for the first time. Dusty celebrated by scoring 91 not out in the first innings before running out of partners. He had been on 60 overnight, when we had three wickets intact, and we all urged him to play some shots in a bid for the maiden century that he has found so elusive. He did just that, and although two wickets went down rapidly, Graham Dilley was staying with him capably. Sadly, Dusty played out a maiden the over before Dilley was out, so had to be content with his seventh score of 90-plus. I had begun to think the game would stick in my mind for nothing more extraordinary than the cane-knife with which the groundstaff cut the wicket each morning, when two regrettable and inter-connected episodes gave the occasion a sour finale.

On the third afternoon a series of decisions by one of the umpires, quaintly named Theodore Brambell, all went against us, and one Leeward batsman, Shirlon Williams, twice survived and failed to 'walk' when our lads were convinced he was out caught – once at short leg and again behind the wicket. Frustrations can easily well up at such moments, and our players did not disguise their feelings. So the following day a debatable l.b.w. decision, this time by Mr Brambell's colleague Pat White, did not leave the victim, Geoff Boycott, in the best of humour.

After making his emotions pretty plain on the field, Fiery stalked back to the dressing-room in high dudgeon. At times like this any batsman just wants to be left alone, and Fiery probably more than most. It was unfortunate that his position in the dressing-room was just behind the door, beside which were some half-open wooden louvres. Just outside, on a bench, sat a group of locals, one of whom had made himself known very loudly throughout the game.

As acting twelfth man for the session I silently offered Geoff a glass of water, which he took. At this moment the vocal gentleman outside – separated from Fiery only by a matter of a foot and the louvres – said something tactless. I still don't know what exactly it was, but Fiery, still visibly upset, told him to shut up, then threw the water through the louvres into his face. The man did not take kindly to such retaliation, and rushed off to pick up the nearest missile he could find. It happened to be a brick and he was advancing menacingly towards the dressing-room door when he was headed off by a police sergeant and led away to cool down.

Alan Smith, misguidedly content with the prospect of a quiet few days on this charmingly peaceful island, arrived back at the ground from the hotel about ninety seconds later and had to defuse the situation with apologies. The local had acted foolishly, but I thought Fiery was wrong to react as he did.

Geoff got angry again the following day – but this time I thought it was justified. We flew out of Montserrat in a small chartered plane, climbing out of the tiny airstrip where landing involves an alarming, last-ditch left turn to miss the sea on one side and the mountains on the other, and arrived in Antigua around teatime. A.C. Smith called the players together and began boarding them into taxis bound for the hotel, ignoring the wives and girlfriends who were standing with us outside the terminal. One or two of us asked whether they could come with us, but A.C. said they had to make their own arrangements. I accept that there was a shortage of taxis and A.C. felt that his responsibility was to the team. Fiery decided that was not good enough, so took his girlfriend, Ann, and went in search of his own taxi. Frankly I wish I had done the same, because by then I was getting tired of the manager's attitude towards the wives. None of them had got in the way during their stay with us, nor pushed themselves forward for any perks. But I for one wanted to travel with my wife and not have her ignored. Alan Smith had said nothing, but it seemed to me that he disapproved of the ladies being there, which created a bad atmosphere for a few days.

Having been rested for the match in Montserrat, I'd had the time to see some of the island's delights. I played the golf course, which is dotted with two-foot-long iguanas which look pretty chilling but are, I'm told, quite harmless; I had a caddie who went by the particularly apt name of Ballhawk – he never lost one! I also visited the Air Recording Studios which, astonishingly for such a remote island, had accommodated as customers in the previous few weeks such pop superstars as Paul McCartney and Stevie Wonder.

But it was a fleeting escape from the tour's pressures, for by the time we landed in Antigua less than forty-eight hours remained before the Fourth Test. We had a night to settle in the beach-side hotel where I felt more relaxed than at any stage of the tour, and then we were embroiled in a match that was as much a national carnival as a Test. It was the first time Antigua had ever stages a Test, and they intended to do it properly. Already that week the islanders had celebrated in style the 'society' wedding of their king, Viv Richards. Now they wanted to celebrate his runs – and had no doubts that they would be given the chance. Our first visit to the Test venue, still rustically known as the Recreation Ground, impressed upon us just how much the occasion meant to everyone. When we arrived for practice on the eve of the game, queues for tickets stretched away from the gates, and squads of labourers were still working furiously inside to complete the massive improvements in time for the morrow.

To have a net, we had to walk out of the far end of the ground from the pavilion, across a road to a stretch of waste land where a pitch had been prepared and a net rigged up behind it. To my amazement, about a thousand people had turned up to watch – at most thirty yards from the bat. Although the pitch was good, it was impossible to bat properly because of the risk of killing fans. But this limited practice session was better than nothing, and we at least knew they were keen to see us play.

It is always important to relax on the afternoon before a big game. Some read, some sleep. This time I decided to take one of the island's glass-bottomed boats out to the reef, where I spent a pleasant hour snorkelling. The boatman's name was Papi, and the next time I saw him was during the match. I was fielding at third man, and he was up in the most raucous section of the cheap stands, blowing a horn while his mates danced and chanted all around him.

The team meeting that night was subdued. We knew, of course, that we were outclassed, and even the great optimists, of which the captain was certainly one, could not dig up enough words of inspiration. Robin Jackman, who was cruelly ruled out of the game by a nagging Achilles tendon injury, made the most sensible point when suggesting that we should make our attack more flexible, giving bowlers spells of only five or six overs before making a change, rather than installing them for a session at a time. In terms of hoping to upset the batsmen, every change has a chance and we had been too stereotyped. Sadly, the point did not strike home. I also had a theory, which I had discussed with Geoff Miller. I felt that our batting order should be changed to split up Gower, Butcher and Botham – all players who like to play strokes with freedom. Peter Willey, I thought, should bat at five. But the idea was not adopted until the second innings, by which time Willey had scored a century from number seven after the almost customary pack-of-cards collapse by our middle order.

Ian won the toss again – three times in three Tests – and chose to bat, changing the pattern set in Trinidad and Barbados. So far as any of us could see there was no reason to put the opposition in, because the wicket looked the best we had seen in the Caribbean – flat, hard, and almost devoid of grass. If it was going to turn at all, we thought, it would be slow and late in the game. Having said that, I'm sure Clive Lloyd would have put us in, because his speed attack is always likely to be most effective on the first morning of a game.

Getting through the first hour, then, was critical. Fiery and I accomplished it without too many alarms, and were both feeling well set when disaster struck. Boycott and run-outs tend to go hand-in-hand, but I had to take all the blame for this particular fiasco. I had pushed Croft through mid-on for two comfortable runs. I took the second fast and called for a third. Fiery yelled, 'No', but I was running to the danger end and thought I could make it. Holding was about to pick up the ball as I set off, and I was fractionally beaten by a superb throw. Looking back, it was a miscalculation and a needless one, because we were certainly not chasing runs and had in fact put on 60 in ninety minutes. Very frustrating. I had been in very little trouble and had even been able to venture on to the front foot to drive, a rare privilege against this attack.

But the pattern set in the previous England innings continued; we lost one wicket, then two more. Bill Athey was quickly out to Croft, and Fiery got a very good ball from the same bowler. From 60 without loss, we were 95 for three and rocking. Midway through the second session three more wickets went down inside four overs, and on a pitch where we had to be looking for a minimum of 350 we were 138 for six. But Willey, who had already batted for a long time in the series without making a major score, produced the goods at the right moment. He got himself right behind the line, defended doggedly as he always does, and also played some strikingly powerful drives in front of the wicket. Will's Test career has never been easy. For as long as I can remember he has had to come in with the innings in tatters and bat unnaturally. He has done the blocking jobs admiringly, but I was delighted to see him take the attack to the bowlers.

John Emburey held up an end for eighty-eight minutes while Peter took us towards a respectable score, once taking three fours in an over from the normally immaculate Garner, and later playing an extraordinary slash over point for six against Croft. By the close we had recovered well to 260 for nine, still far from formidable but at least something to bowl at. Will was on 91 and Picca stayed with him long enough the next morning for him to complete his second Test 100. The last four wickets had virtually doubled our total which, notwithstanding Will's contribution, was a comment on the placid pitch. We should have made a lot more, of that there was no question. We totalled 271, and 100 more would just about have been acceptable. Three of us – Fiery, Lulu and myself – were out in the thirties when set well. If we had only gone on to make sixties, it would have made all the difference.

We were cheered by Botham dismissing Haynes with a very good delivery in his first over, but the rest of the day was torture. Richards and Greenidge began by pounding everything in sight to the boundary – the first 32 runs came in fours – but after lunch they settled into a mood of caution. Both looked intent on a long innings, Greenidge because he had twice failed in Barbados, and Richards because everyone demanded it of him. Greenidge got himself out at 63, driving Stevenson straight to mid-on, but Richards and Everton Mattis batted through to the close. Our lead was down to 35 and they had lost only two wickets.

Despite Jackers' remarks at the team meeting, which had been generally approved, Ian still declined to change the bowling other than in rigid patterns. We had off-spin from one end for four hours, and although both Emburey and Willey bowled tidily, the batsmen were able to get into a groove against them. My other gripe was that we ignored the new ball when it became due with just under half an hour left. I simply could not understand it. Mattis, to my mind, must always be vulnerable when the ball swings at all because he is so right-handed. Fielding at slip to him, you imagine the ball is coming to you every time he shapes to drive. And Richards, despite having taken the new ball apart in Barbados at a similar time of day, was in his shell and playing for the close. It might just have disturbed him. Surely it was worth a try? Ian told me later that he had not wanted to give Viv the chance to cut loose, as he had done in the previous Test. He knew I had been upset on the field, and I did not change my opinion. Perhaps we had done well to contain them to 236 in five hours – but the lads were certainly very low that night. Logically, we had little to look forward to in the game.

It just shows how wrong you can be. By lunch on the third day the West Indies were 301 for seven, with only Lloyd left of the recognized batsmen. Picca had taken the new ball immediately, conceded a four second ball to an audacious shot from Richards, then removed him two deliveries later as he went impulsively for the hook. Botham then turned in his best spell of the tour, taking three wickets for one in a five-ball burst. Roberts was out to Stevenson and the whole game had been turned on its head. We were thinking that they might score 500, but at lunch we had revived so dramatically that we could realistically hope for a deficit of no more than 60.

The optimism was short-lived. Ninety-nine runs were scored between lunch and tea, and Lloyd's was the only wicket to fall. Finally, as we continued to fail embarrassingly in efforts to remove the tail, Lloyd was able to declare at 468 for nine and get us in for the final half-hour of the day. It is impossible to budget for Joel Garner scoring 46 and Michael Holding 58 not out. They batted well, we bowled with no great fire, and the wicket was so good that they were able to play in great comfort. The morning's good work had gone to waste and they had piled up almost as big a score as we had originally feared. Much more humiliating, they had done so through the last couple of batsmen.

So we were back in the familiar position of having to bat two days to save the game. Bad light came to our aid that evening, allowing the bowlers only four overs, and the weather turned obligingly nasty on the rest day which followed. It rained for most of the day and the wind howled as it does on the Yorkshire moors in February, so perhaps John Emburey was a little unwise when he took out one of the miniature sailing dinghies that could be hired from near the hotel. He had not sailed much before, and whereas Mike Gatting chose to take his boat back when the sea became rough, Embers carried on and found himself in real difficulties. He shouted and whistled for help when he found he could not turn the boat round, and he later admitted he was frightened – as most of us would have been – by the time Papi and his glass-bottomed launch went out to the rescue.

After that alarm, however, we were all happy to see the rain continue. Although the next day dawned hot and sunny there were enough wet patches on the wicket, where the covers had leaked, to delay the start even before the skies darkened and opened mid-morning. It was obvious to most of us after the second of four heavy showers that there would be no play, but the umpires insisted on waiting until 4 p.m. before abandoning hope. It was one of those dressing-room days that every English cricketer gets used to at home, yet never quite expects abroad. Five of our lads played cards almost all day. Some took the chance to sleep on the two double beds which, unusually, decorated the new dressing-rooms. I just sat and read, finishing *The Day of the Jackal* and starting on my third Frederick Forsyth of the tour.

While the loss of a complete day had obviously done our chances of survival no harm, we felt some apprehension about the state of the pitch when it was eventually passed as playable. The fears remained the following morning, for the patches were still visible, although now baked dry by the sun. We need not have worried: play began on time, and the wicket was as amiable as it had been throughout the game. It had, in fact, lost some of its pace and bounce and the ball never deviated at all. Although Croft worked up a great pace, he was not able to bowl the devastating leg-cutters which had made him such an awesome proposition earlier. I felt that if we got through to lunch without losing a wicket we must be fancied to save the game. In fact we went a little better: Fiery and I put on 144 in three hours before I got out for 83, with a second century in successive Tests there for the asking. Viv Richards had been brought on to bowl, mainly to give the pacemen a breather, and I decided it was worth attacking against him. It is not every day you can indulge in some stroke play against the West Indies; against the fast bowlers you merely accumulate, if you are lucky. I moved rapidly from 50 to 83, hitting six fours, then mistimed an on-drive as Richards held one back a little.

Fiery stayed, and played well in characteristic style; he reached his century just before the close and England eventually saved the game in some comfort. It must have done his confidence good – he had twice been out inside an over in Barbados, and the usual mutterings about slowing reactions had been heard. He worked hard for his runs but looked as secure as ever. Bill Athey failed again, making only one and continuing England's extraordinary run of flops at number three. In this series three men had been tried in the position, and their scores read ten, five, two, nought, two and one. It was difficult to know where to turn next, but I hoped Bill would be given another chance. Even though the game ended in the result that we wanted, it was still an unsatisfactory match. We should have done so much better after winning the toss, as our second-innings efforts emphasized. And despite the draw we had now officially lost the series. Our wives went home that night, and I'm quite certain there were a number of players who looked wistfully after the British Airways jumbo as it left Coolidge Airport. I know I would like to have been on it.

As it was, I returned to David Gower's birthday party in a house near our hotel, where somebody dropped a comment which left me feeling rather alarmed at an apparently strange encounter. While in Barbados I had got to know a man called John Miller, a Scot who had a yacht in the harbour. I had a couple of drinks with him one night, and the next day he invited Geoff Miller and me on board. We stayed for almost an hour and enjoyed the hospitality of Mr Miller and his friends. He told me they were sailing to Brazil in a week or two to do some filming around the oil rigs. I thanked him for his kindness and thought no more about him – until that night at the party. A group of us were discussing the kidnap of the Great Train Robber Ronald Biggs from his Brazilian hideaway. Apparently he had been snatched by a gang of bounty hunters, held on a yacht and taken to Barbados, where he was now facing an extradition order. The name of the kidnappers' leader, I was reliably informed, was John Miller, my friendly Scotsman.

7

Guards, Guns and Runs

Kingston, Jamaica, one of the world's most violent cities, was an unwelcome last leg to this torrid tour. Despite the reputed calm which had settled over the island following the recent change of government, it was reported that more than 400 people had been shot dead in the streets inside five months — figures to deter any casual tourist and fill every cricketer with apprehension.

Stirring up the hostile brew was the legacy of the Guyana crisis. Jamaica, racially sensitive, was not expected to throw its arms unanimously wide for Robin Jackman, and even before the team's arrival news of pressure groups threatening disruptive protests filtered through, together with a planned 'black list' from SANROC, the South African anti-apartheid organization, which would include Geoff Boycott but, paradoxically, not Jackman. The mood, understandably, was anything but jolly as the squad flew into Norman Manley Airport, Kingston, on the afternoon of 2 April.

We were two steps out of the airport when I saw the guns — great, heavy machine-guns, rifles and pistols, all being worn by the deadpan uniformed policeman sent there to protect us. Knowing the situation, I should not have been surprised — but I confess it alarmed me. Looking round, and listening to the chatter, I knew it had affected the rest of the boys too. It was just as well that an ill-informed local released the tension by poking his head through the window of the minibus and sizing up the features and balding head of Bernard Thomas before saying to his own satisfaction and our amusement: 'You, Boycott!'

A twenty-minute drive to the hotel awaited us, and we

were not alone. Two Land Rovers crammed with police escorted us through the suburbs of Kingston, past a few of the grimier downtown areas to the more cosmopolitan new town, where the blue and white of the eighteen-storey Pegasus Hotel greeted us. The vehicle in front kept the rear door open throughout the journey, and one of the guards sat on sentry, his sten-gun poised. It was an extraordinary experience, and it was far from finished. Another posse of police was stationed outside the hotel, and yet more in the lobby, their weapons obvious to all. What the other guests thought, I can't imagine – but perhaps they were more used to it than we were.

Security arrangements, I understand, are always fairly strict for visiting teams in Kingston. For us, with the prevailing scent of trouble around us, they had been doubled at least. Three guards were allotted to us twenty-four hours a day. Roland, the chief, Arthur and Billy policed our floor of the hotel, armed with radios as well as guns. Everywhere we went, they followed, and everyone who tried to come on to our floor was looked at and, if necessary, stopped. On the first day these precautions produced a moment of supreme farce. Alan Smith's manager's suite was on the fourteenth floor, seven up from the rest of us. When he arrived on the seventh to sort out some arrangements with us the guard refused to let him past, disbelieving his protests that he was the England manager. Poor A.C. had fallen foul of his own security plans!

The Land Rover escorts were used every time we left the hotel as a team. If we went out in groups, to the golf course for instance, a couple of guards would go with us, swapping their red and blue uniforms for civilian clothes. During one round of golf Roland decided that his gun – a Browning automatic – was getting rusty through lack of use, so he fired a shot into a gully to the side of a fairway. It was a strange sensation to see someone do that, and know what the weapon's real purpose was. I had held a gun only once in my life, and had seldom even seen a real one.

There was no doubt, however, that guns were essential police equipment in Kingston, where street violence appeared to be accepted, however reluctantly, as part of everyday life. It was impossible to pick up a local paper without reading headlines about horrifying shootings. We had been there only four days when the evening paper lead story told of fifteen gunmen firing indiscriminately into a crowd on a street corner in town late the previous night. Two had been killed, many more injured. The second story, no more comforting, was about a man chopped to death by civilians who had found him attacking his seventy-year-old father with a machete. In our first week in Kingston at least twenty people must have been murdered in the city's streets, and it was nothing unusual.

Downtown Kingston is grubby and menacing, and even the locals warned us never to walk there alone. We did not need telling twice. A.C. had, in fact, repeated his warning given at Georgetown: no one was to leave the hotel at night, except for official functions. It really didn't matter, because there was nowhere we wanted to go. The Pegasus was spacious and comfortable, with good food and several bars. Most of us found we could live there perfectly comfortably, with boredom and monotony the only enemies. By nature I am not a card player – in fact I find it unsociable at times – but for five consecutive nights in Kingston I joined a card school playing Hearts – not for money, but just to while away the hours. I was easily the worst player! I was in bed early every night: once I went at eight o'clock, but wished I hadn't when I was awake before five the following morning.

There was no doubt that we all wanted to go home. It is a natural feeling at the end of every tour, because three months away from one's wife and family is hard to accept. But this time too much had gone wrong; the buoyancy had been sucked out of us, and if we could have wished away those final two weeks and climbed straight on board the flight home, I don't believe anyone would have hesitated. But of course we couldn't. There were two matches left, and somehow we had to lift ourselves for them. For the Test it would be easier, because we still had our pride and professionalism. We wanted to win one or, if that was impossible, at least stop them going three–nil ahead. But first we had to play Jamaica in our final four-day fixture, and I have to admit I made a poor job of motivating myself.

I had reached 31 on the opening morning when I threw my wicket away – I attacked the off-spinner Richard Austin with no great control and was stumped. I can only explain this rush of blood by saying I was bored, and I am perfectly aware that was the wrong attitude. It was a bad example to set the younger players, especially as I had been preaching to them about making the most of every innings you play. At least it brought me sharply to my senses, and I was determined to do nothing similar in the second innings. Thankfully, I redeemed myself with a century and thoroughly enjoyed the challenge – unusual for this tour – of batting against three spinners bowling in helpful conditions. It was a battle of wits, as opposed to the battle for survival to which I had grown accustomed after a year of Tests against the West Indies' attack, and while it might not have been the most orthodox form of preparation for the final Test it made me feel good.

The game was remarkable for the number of invalids in our camp. Geoff Miller had a virus and Graham Stevenson a thigh strain, so they were not even considered, and by the second day the sick list included Chris Old, who pulled a muscle early in his new-ball spell, Geoff Boycott with laryngitis, and Paul Downton who was another virus victim. When John Emburey briefly went off the field to have a bruised knee strapped our resources had run dry, and much to everyone's amusement A.C. had to come on as our fourth substitute. For some reason he declined to field at bat-pad when Ian offered it to him!

This was the third of the four-day games which died on its feet, not even entering its fourth innings, and there was some media criticism of us for not declaring midway through the final afternoon and setting Jamaica a target of around 250. To me, such a move would have been no more than a gesture to the locals, because the wicket was too good for us to have any reasonable hope of bowling them out inside three hours. I felt that we could have declared at teatime, just to make a show of giving the home side another innings and the crowd another chance to watch their idol Lawrence Rowe bat; but on balance perhaps it was of more benefit to us to give players like Gatting and Butcher another long airing at the crease. Rowe, whose career has been plagued by minor injuries and ailments ever since his triple century against the MCC team of 1973–4, showed what a great player he remains by scoring an elegant century in their only innings. For my money he is still a far better player than one or two in the current West Indies middle order.

What surprised me most about this match was Sabina Park itself. When I was last there, nine years earlier, I remembered it as a tiny ground with a great deal of atmosphere, the playing area surrounded by low wooden stands, the boundaries small, and the crowd apparently close enough to shake hands. Not any more. The quaint old stands all along the south side of the ground had disappeared, and in their place was a massive, three-tier concrete stand. It would have been immensely impressive but for the fact that the project was a little behind schedule. Like all the best Spanish holiday hotels, it was only half-finished. Our dressing-rooms, at ground level, were no more than concrete shells containing some metal chairs. You stepped straight out of the back door on to the building site, treading through dirt and rubble and holding your nose against the stench of things unknown.

Even in such primitive surroundings, however, we were never deserted by the guards. There were dozens of them posted either side of the dressing-rooms, and 270 policemen in all were on duty to control the crowds at the Jamaica match. The numbers were to be doubled for the Test. As it turned out, the threats of disruption were hollow and puny. The one political group to declare themselves was an organization called the Ad-Hoc Committee against Apartheid. The group had been formed specifically to protest about Robin Jackman and make 'peaceful demonstrations' against the staging of the Test.

Its inaugural meeting, held in a dingy club not far from the team hotel, attracted an audience of 130 people, but their planned demo on the opening day of the Test was a feeble affair involving about twenty people distributing leaflets outside the ground. The rest of Jamaica, it appeared, were perfectly content to see the Test go on, with or without Jackers.

The Ad-Hoc Committee did, however, issue an extraordinary statement which would no doubt have been libellous on several points if Jackers had felt like taking it seriously. It stated unequivocally that Robin 'agrees with apartheid' and said: '. . . there is no doubt that Jackman is a white racist and a hater of black people'. Working themselves into something of a lather, the Ad-Hoc crew then claimed that '. . . the Jamaican government has insulted the majority of the Jamaican people by allowing Jackman to come here', and finished with a hysterical plea: 'Would you make your children play with a white racist, a hater of black people? Or would you isolate the racist? . . . Boycott the Test Match. Show your disgust at racism and apartheid. Jackman must not play a Test Match here.' This strange group had such an effect on the people of Jamaica that on the Saturday and Sunday of the Test the Sabine Park crowd record was twice broken. What is more, Jackers – who had understandably been worried about the reception he might be given – was warmly greeted, and became a crowd favourite when he started acting up with mimes and gestures. Caribbean crowds love to feel involved with the players, and they cheered Robin's every move, down to his last theatrical appeal. Clearly they cared nothing for the views of the Ad-Hoc Committee.

Our build-up to the Test was inevitably not quite in the same gear as for the earlier games. At the team meeting on the Thursday evening Ian tried to instil in us the importance of going out on a high note, with either a win or a creditable draw. There was no point in going through their players again – we had been up against most of them non-stop for almost a year now, and if we didn't know how they played now we probably never would. But we tried at least to be positive. Team selection was not, I imagine, a difficult business. With Graham Stevenson and Chris Old both injured, the bowlers picked themselves, and the one contentious batting position was retained by Butcher despite Gatting's 93 and 42 against Jamaica. The West Indies made their first team change of the series, and it may well have marked the end of a distinguished Test career. Andy Roberts, at thirty the oldest and most experienced of the four quick bowlers, was dropped to make way for his Hampshire successor, Malcolm Marshall. Andy had not recently been as lively as of old, and it was not a surprising move. Marshall is deceptively quick; because he is so much shorter than the others he tends to skid the ball through, and he is very effective in British conditions because he generally keeps the ball well up to the bat.

There had been a lot of advance discussion about the Sabina Park pitch. Most people had speculated that it would be grassy, giving the quick bowlers a lot of help on the first day, but when we arrived at the ground it was in fact not as green as we had feared. Ian asked each of the senior players what they thought England should do if he won the toss for the fourth time in the series. Although it would have been a more attacking move to bat first and use whatever turn might be available late in the game, I felt the West Indians might easily bowl us out if the wicket misbehaved, so I was in favour of putting them in. The majority agreed, but the decision never had to be taken because Lloyd at last won a toss and, as expected, gave his bowlers first use of the pitch.

To my surprise, Marshall was given the new ball in preference to Croft, who had not only taken more wickets but achieved more bounce than any of the other bowlers in the series. But the pitch was nothing like as evil as had been predicted, and although there was some uneven bounce, with short balls tending to keep low, it was certainly not dangerous, and Fiery and I made a very satisfying start. By lunch 93 runs were on the board at almost four an over. The next session cost us three wickets, irritating because two batsmen – Bill Athey and David Gower – were bowled round their legs, something which might happen once a season. Fiery had gone first, and although it was another of the good, lifting deliveries which appeared to be following him around, I felt again that he had got a little too low, and followed the ball with his hands.

For me it was a memorable session. I moved from 46 to 124 and batted better than I have ever done for England. It was a very different century from the one I had scored in Barbados, where survival was the priority. Here I had decided to play my natural game, and if any ball was short and wide of off-stump I would attack it rather than shouldering arms. I felt that if I struck it properly it would go for four, and if I edged it it might fly hard and high enough to clear the slips. Croft gave me plenty of chance to test the theory, bowling much too short. To my great satisfaction his first four overs cost 33 runs, and his next four a further 23, including a six which I steered deliberately over the slip cordon and third man.

After reaching 100 I consciously settled myself again. This time I was not going to be satisfied. I still had too much of a reputation for not turning good innings into major ones, so I thought again of Ken Barrington's words, forced myself to concentrate, and played myself in for another couple of hours. I was eventually out for 153 after more than five hours, my longest and most fulfilling Test innings – also, without question, my most tiring. I can never remember feeling so hot for so long. The temperature was above 90 degrees and it was stiflingly humid. My hands were sweating so much that I had to change my batting gloves every forty-five minutes because they were sliding off the bat handle. But although I was very happy that evening I knew we had not made the most of what could have been our first dominant day in the series. We had scored 278 runs, a marvellous rate considering the West Indies had bowled only 78 overs, but we had lost six wickets, which was at least two too many. The following morning was to be crucial: we needed another 100 runs, and that meant surviving the second new ball, which was due any time Clive Lloyd chose to take it.

Lloyd chose to take the new ball immediately, and England did not survive very long. It took half an hour, in fact, for our last four wickets to tumble, three of them to Michael Holding, who appeared to bowl quicker than at any stage of the first day. He also found a spot from which the ball would fly disconcertingly, and Jackman in particular took some nasty blows on the hand. England were all out for 285 and under no illusions about what that meant. Gordon Greenidge and Desmond Haynes rubbed in the point with a century stand for their first wicket, and although our bowlers never allowed them the freedom to play as aggressively as they would have liked, the wicket continued to look full of runs and our score looked smaller by the minute.

Graham Dilley had run in well for his opening spell and bowled with the hostility needed from him. However he was only midway through his fifth over when the heel of one of his boots came off, the result of the dragged right foot which is such a noticeable part of his action. I could not blame him for the mishap, which could happen to any quick bowler, but I was dismayed that his only other pair of bowling boots had been left back at the hotel, and we were reduced to making a tannoy plea for a cobbler to repair the damaged one. This deprived us of our main strike bowler for a considerable period, and was frankly quite unprofessional. Equipment and its care are a vital part of every sportsman's job. I only hope the incident taught Graham something.

For the rest of the day we could only try to contain. Picca came back well, shod with repaired boots, and dismissed both Greenidge and Richards – the fourth time he had taken Viv's wicket on the tour. But Haynes ground his way onwards and had batted almost five hours when he was yorked by Peter Willey for 84 shortly before the close. John Emburey was again the subject of sympathy. Coming on from the pavilion end early in the innings, he had bowled right through to the close – 31 overs for 54 runs, and not a single wicket to recognize just how impeccable he had been. So often in this series Embers had to come on when the wicket was not in his favour and run saving was at least as important as wicket taking. Every time he had performed admirably; yet the statistics never showed how well he bowled.

The locals were probably scenting victory. On Sunday they turned up in such numbers that the legendary tales of West Indian crowds hanging from trees, telegraph poles and scaffolding were all proved true. There were more than 20,000 inside Sabina Park, but if they came for excitement they were disappointed. It was a day of West Indian consolidation – 249 runs in 85 overs, to give them a first-innings lead of 157. Most of the runs came from Lloyd and Larry Gomes, 95 and 90 not out respectively. Clive had been a major influence throughout the series; every time the West Indies' innings looked like wobbling, Lloyd would be there, and he never once failed to make 50. Gomes is a very untypical batsman for a West Indies side. He likes to accumulate runs quietly, just occasionally expressing himself with a flowing cover drive, but never batting with the explosive power of a Greenidge or a Richards. He complements these players well, because he plays a steadying role to offset the stroke players' extravagances.

For much of the day England had two substitutes on the field. Butcher had pulled a groin muscle in the field, and Boycott, who had complained of feeling ill early in the morning, retired to bed after being sick at lunchtime. We finished the day as we had finished several third days during the series, with only survival to play for. At this late stage of a fraught tour a rest day could have been tedious – but not this one. After a round of golf on the Constant Springs course in the morning, nine of us paid an invited visit to the para-military police training camp. For several hours we enjoyed ourselves on the target ranges, trying each of the different guns carried by the Jamaican police – every one of which we had been alarmed to see at such close quarters in the preceding fortnight. Ian Botham, a shooting enthusiast in England, and Robin Jackman turned out to be better shots than a number of our personal guards. After failing to master the Browning and the Smith & Wesson, I managed to score nine out of ten with the sub-machine-gun and eighteen out of twenty with an M16 rifle. The latter weapon was the one responsible for many of the reported deaths during our time in Kingston; its ability to fire through a half-inch-thick steel plate at 100 yards range was demonstrated to us.

Two days remained; two days in which to salvage some pride, or go down like the sinking ship to which we had already been likened in the press. It could hardly have looked worse for us when three wickets fell in the opening hour of the fourth day. It was the most devastating start we had suffered in the series, because both Boycott and I were among the dismissals. The third was Bill Athey, caught behind off Holding while playing no shot, and no doubt walking back to the dressing-room sickened by the thought that his total from six Test innings was now 17 runs. He is a better player than that, and I only hope he can conquer his nerves, iron out a few weaknesses and show an improvement.

David Gower has done just that. Written off as irresponsible not so long before, he had enjoyed a splendid tour, apparently a much improved player. But up to now he had not played the big Test innings to prove his point: the stage was set, and he did not waste the chance. For eight hours, the longest innings he had ever played, Lulu defied everything the West Indians could concoct to bowl at him. He finished exhausted but very satisfied, his 154 not out making up for all his frustrations earlier in the series. As I knew only too well, feeling in good form yet continually getting out in the thirties is somehow worse than playing badly and not making runs. But Gower, to his great credit, exercised all the discipline he had added to his game, and at last reaped the benefits. Peter Willey stayed with him for three hours, adding to the reputation he had gained on this tour, and Paul Downton – desperately short of runs up to then – played out the last three overs, not always comfortably but with a great deal of pluck.

Survival was eventually achieved without drama or the need for nail biting. Four wickets stood at the end, and the joke bowlers had been on for some time. The wicket, subject of so much apprehensive talk, had stayed fairly true to the death, and if only we had made more runs in the first innings we might have been in a challenging position. The story of the tour: if only. . . .

8

Reflections on a Torrid Tour

It was over – perhaps the most fated and the unhappiest England tour of all time. One player, David Gower, went to Barbados for a holiday. The other fifteen survivors, together with Alan Smith and Bernard Thomas and the press corps, spent a further forty-eight hours in their Kingston hotel before boarding a British Airways TriStar bound for Heathrow. They had been away ninety-three days, and to most of them it seemed very much longer. The achievements had been minor in terms of results, and the advances made by half a dozen players had to be set against the disasters suffered by others. They returned with many questions still unanswered, paramount among them being Ian Botham's future as a Test captain.

Everyone enjoys complaining about his job now and again: cricketers are frequently cynical about tours in which most people would love to have taken part. This one, however, was different: I could not with hand on heart claim that I enjoyed it, and I cannot believe that many of the others did either. A lengthy list could be drawn up of the setbacks and catastrophes which befell us, and even the most imaginative scriptwriter would reject the plot as far-fetched. To lose two senior players after a month and lose the series comprehensively would have been enough to tarnish the trip. A pitch sabotage, a political crisis and the stunning death of a man loved by all were too much.

Deep down, I had always known that to beat the West Indies we would need to play better than ever before.

They had too many big guns for us, and on their own
territory I don't think any other side in the world today
could have coped with them. I had hoped, however, that
we might hold our own by playing to the peak of our
potential. Even in that we failed, because we did not once
play collectively at our best. Four players – Boycott,
Gower, Willey and myself – batted well at various stages
of the series, but there was never more than one substantial individual contribution in an innings. Two at least
were needed if England were to reach 350, the minimum
required to give our bowlers a figure to attack, but we
never managed that many. In fact we only passed 300
once, and that was in the final innings of the series, when
survival was all and runs were virtually irrelevant.

The West Indian bowlers, as we had feared, held the
key. They bowled us out on all types of wickets, good and
bad, proving themselves perhaps the most potent of all
pace attacks, simply because there was never any escape
from them. Many people have criticized the policy of
playing four fast bowlers, even claiming that it is killing
the game. Say what you like, it certainly makes effective
cricket, and in this series Colin Croft was probably the
most effective of all. At Trinidad, in the First Test, he
contrived to cut the ball bewilderingly at high speed, and
throughout the tour he was capable of bowling spells
twenty minutes longer than any of the others. His stamina
was startling, and he seemed to thrive on work. Michael
Holding was the other spearhead. A more lithe and
athletic figure than Croft, he relies extensively on his pace.
If he is not feeling right, and cannot generate speed,
he will probably not get the batsman out. But in this
series he bowled two or three devastating spells, and one
sensed he always had the ability to bowl the unplayable
delivery.

The England players became depressed and deflated
through constantly fighting for survival. In twelve months
we had played nine Tests against this attack, and apart
from the first at Trent Bridge they all followed a similar
pattern: England failing to make enough runs, the West

Indies establishing a lead, England battling for the draw. It is easy to be wise with hindsight, but our tour party certainly seemed badly balanced. Once Brian Rose had been flown home there was no cover for the openers and no obvious candidate at number three. Bill Athey, a promising young player, was not the experienced head we needed. Ideally, I believe we should have taken four men who could open the innings.

Our bowling lacked variety. After Willis' departure, Graham Dilley was the only man with any pace, and he still needs a year or two to mature into a genuine Test new-ball operator. Admirably as John Emburey bowled, he never had a wicket which offered much turn, so he was consistently faced with a purely defensive role. Nevertheless, I believe a left-arm spinner should have gone instead of one of the off-spinners. Choosing the Test wicketkeeper became another problem. Paul Downton ended the trip with the job, but for much of the time neither he nor David Bairstow knew where they stood. Downton had kept well in the First Test, and was left out when the selectors decided Bairstow might make more runs. That policy in turn was abandoned after one match, when Downton was recalled. Paul impressed me with his keeping, but if he is to become established in Test cricket I feel he must improve his batting.

Geoff Boycott's contributions were as dependable as ever; his reactions, the subject of so much fanciful theorizing, appeared to have got only slightly slower, if at all. Just occasionally we saw his notorious side, the irritating quirks in his character which can upset others, but generally he was a constant, steady factor. He made his runs, practised fervently and disappeared in the evenings. Fiery never mixes with the rest of the team, and never has. There is no point in trying to change him.

Roland Butcher had set off under a glaring spotlight, followed by awful predictions of victimization and crowd hatred, all of which proved completely unjustified. Everywhere we went the locals loved him, and although they passionately supported their own side I got the

Hot work in Trinidad, as I take a moment's relaxation during my century against the island side

A century in Barbados, and an English supporter found his way out to the middle to shake my hand. My natural joy was tempered; Ken Barrington had died two days earlier

Another boundary against Trinidad, watched by wicketkeeper Derek Murray, whose omission from the Test side caused demonstrations and boycotts on his home island

Far left The captain, identified by his medallion, seeks refreshment during a training session in Barbados

Left When it rained in Guyana, we kept fit in any way possible – and that included frequent games of tennis on the hotel courts

Below left There were some good times in the Caribbean. Snorkelling with Mike Gatting and John Emburey was great fun

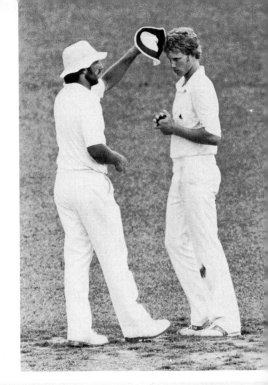

Right Graham Dilley and Ian Botham had their quarrels in the West Indies, and neither looks delighted with affairs here

Below Robin Jackman's ordeal is over, and with manager Alan Smith – still looking grim – in the background, he conducts a press conference at our Bridgetown hotel

A joke, and perhaps a few words,
shared by two great competitors.
Botham and Lillee at Old Trafford

Botham has lost the captaincy but
turned the series. He relaxes in the
Headingley dressing room with a
celebratory cigar after his astonishing

Four to fine leg for me at Leeds during the one-day series we managed to lose to Australia

Left Virtually the end of the summer series for me. Leg before to Dennis Lillee and the moment I knew I would surely be dropped

Rod Marsh swoops, the bails fly and Ian Botham looks anguished. But his back foot is entrenched and he survives, during his second century of the Ashes series

Right India's captain and master batsman, Sunil Gavaskar. Gatting takes evasive action

An unusual show of temper from 'Fletch', taking out his frustration on the stumps after a controversial dismissal at Delhi

Allan Border consistently appeared to be the Australians' most courageous and accomplished batsman

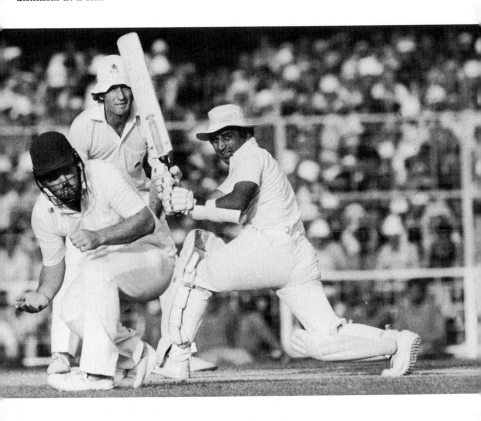

I achieved the first hole-in-one of my golfing life at Calcutta, but needless to say this was not the memorable shot

Drinks breaks are frequent, prolonged, but necessary in India. A bottle each for the captain and myself

An unhappy figure, alone and silent. The story of Geoff Boycott's short tour

Left Not quite like the commuter line to Liverpool Street. Keith Fletcher and I plus interested onlookers from the platform during our trip to Ahmedabad

Looking more like a music-hall figure, but in fact the man we agreed to be the best of India's Test umpires, the massive frame of Swaroop Kishan

Left Bob Willis, hostile as ever, looks as if he is about to strike Vengsarkar again; in fact he is offering help after knocking him out

Brenda arrived straight after Christmas, and the tour brightened

impression they all wanted Butch to make runs. Sadly he disappointed them, never making a big score in the Tests. I felt he was confusing himself with theories about how he should bat in Tests. He was picked as an aggressor, in the hope that he would play even one explosive innings which might just demoralize the opposition for a while. But he changed his game, went into his shell, and never once batted in the manner which gained him selection. Off the field Butch was another loner, like Boycott, Brian Rose, and up to a point Peter Willey. One rarely saw them at night. Butch's solitude had nothing whatever to do with his colour – in the dressing-room, indeed, he was lively and amusing – but he simply wanted to spend his evenings alone, either reading or writing up his diary in his room, or taking in yet another film at the cinema which is one of his great loves.

While Boycott and Butcher were always going to be controversial figures on the tour, few expected Peter Willey to make news. He had always been a fringe player, struggling to do enough to keep his place, and I for one was delighted that he established himself so securely, despite having to bat under enormous pressure almost every time he went to the crease. I grew to know him well on tour, since we roomed together in Guyana and Jamaica, the two places where there was simply nothing to do in the evenings. We worked out our lives quite comfortably, sharing our music tapes and our drink and generally going to bed early with a book. Peter is quiet to the point of being strikingly silent. But he is a strong man in terms of character and physical power, and none of the tour jokers took any liberties with him. He spent most of his spare time in his room and liked to eat very early, read until about nine, and then go to sleep. By the end of the trip I think he was looking forward more than anyone to going home, but he retained his good sense of humour and remained a steadying influence on the spirit and performance of the team.

The funny man of the side was certainly Graham Stevenson. He kept everyone amused, even at times of crisis, and was never short of something to say in his broad South Yorkshire accent. The pity of it was that he did not advance as a player. Steve has a lot of ability, but is still too erratic; the next five years should logically be his best, if he makes the most of his talent. The rest of the squad I have already talked about at various points. I was delighted for Robin Jackman, disappointed in Chris Old, and sad for Bob Willis, who might have been a great help to the captain and to Dilley. I felt sorry for Mike Gatting and Geoff Miller, who had so little opportunity, and elated for David Gower, now truly a world-class player.

For Ian Botham my feelings were mixed. He came home with the critics howling for his head and suggesting any other name as a replacement. That in itself was unfair, because no one alive could have changed the result of this series with the players Ian had available. However, his own performances with bat and ball were dismally short of the standards we had all come to expect from him. He did take more wickets than anyone else in the England side, and chiefly on wickets unhelpful to his bowling. But I did not feel he was as dangerous as the Botham of eighteen months earlier. His batting record was almost embarrassing – 73 runs in seven Test innings – but it was the style of it which disturbed me more. Somehow he seemed unable to adapt his game to difficult situations and at times he played reckless strokes, which, if I had not known him better, I would have put down to lack of determination.

Some of the young players were hard put to retain their regard for a leader who did such irresponsible things, and although Ian never visibly appeared to worry about himself, I am sure the pressure got through to him. He said towards the end of the tour that he was enjoying the job much more, because he understood it better. Yet in my opinion he still fitted each player into a category, without delving into minds and personalities to see what made individuals tick. But, as I said, it was a tough tour, and no one envied Ian his job. He came home to personal problems, including an appearance in court charged with assault, and a newspaper story about a fracas with journalist Henry Blofeld at Bermuda Airport on the way home. Trouble, it seems, follows Ian Botham around.

9

Botham on a Tightrope

There was to be no respite. Three days after arriving home Gooch joined the Essex squad for pre-season training, and within another week he was playing again, in the first major match of the year for MCC against the champions. If he was a celebrity of sorts before the tour, he was now publicly recognized as a star. With that recognition came greater attention and inevitable pressure.

The question almost everybody asks me at the end of a tour is whether I enjoyed myself: harmless, certainly, but in this case I found it dreadfully difficult to answer. I could not honestly say I had a good time, despite the fact that the majority of people I know would have given a great deal for their idea of three months in the Caribbean. That image, however, was very far from the truth. The calamities made it a wearing trip on which it was often difficult to show much jollity. It was strange, looking back, that the things we were afraid might happen – crowd riots, racial unpleasantness and serious injuries caused by the West Indian quick bowlers – did not transpire at all. But just about everything else you could conceive of went wrong.

For all that I had done well, and it would not have been right to put on an agonized face and pretend it was endless torture. I was pleased to be home, and I left it at that.

Some players find it difficult to readjust to being at home after the routine of living in a hotel and having their lives organized by others. I have no such problem, and I looked forward to nothing more than sitting at home with Brenda for a few nights, just watching television. There were not many such idle evenings ahead of me, though: the tour had ended too close to the start of the home season for that. There was no time to think of a holiday, and precious little time to tackle some of the domestic jobs which always mount up. I wanted to do some more decorating in our new home, but that had to wait for rainy days. My diary quickly filled up for the weeks ahead. I was asked to speak at dinners, coach boys in indoor nets and even open a new kitchen shop! It is impossible to accept every invitation, but I do take on as many engagements as my timetable, energy and wife can stand.

Essex's first fixture of the season was at Cambridge, against the University, on 22 April. We had been back in England four days, so I was excused duty, but on the first morning I decided to make the short journey up the M11 to be there; the last thing I wanted was to be thought a prima donna. I should have known better; having made known my intentions to run around Parker's Piece, I was promptly given a shopping list. Ray East, known around the cricket circuit as a master of goonish comedy, ordered a quarter pound of winter mixtures – a comment on just how bitingly cold an April day it was – and John Lever asked for some pork pies to supplement the ham salad lunch. When I jogged back into the ground, clad in thick sweaters and tracksuit plus blue commando bobble hat, Essex had been in the field for half an hour, and John – having taken a wicket with the first delivery of the new season – insisted on sampling one of the pork pies on the boundary, an event which was captured by an alert photographer and featured prominently in the following day's papers.

Such light-hearted moments are common in Essex cricket and have helped the county build a name as a team of characters who obviously enjoy the game. We are lucky to have players with enough personality to achieve the humorous and unexpected without strain, but it is also true that such an overtly relaxed atmosphere helps any young and slightly overawed newcomer as he tries to settle into the side. Beneath the veneer is a strong will to win. After Essex's double in 1979 – the Championship and Benson & Hedges Cup – 1980 had been a relative anticlimax, and the team were determined to prove that they had not passed their best as a unit. We trained hard, under the guidance of John Lever, and even those players who are not naturally versatile athletes took the job seriously.

The Chelmsford ground had undergone considerable winter improvements. A new scoreboard had replaced the well-known converted caravan which travelled the Essex grounds for so many years, and terraces of coloured seats had been constructed where grass banks had previously given a quaint but unprofessional look to one side of the ground. The place now looked a proper, smart county ground rather than the overgrown park it had been before, but the developments had been done tastefully enough to retain its character.

I met some of the touring party again at a benefit golf match for Bob Willis, held just south of Birmingham. I do not claim to be among the world's best golfers, and at the second hole I contrived to lose two new balls by screwing drives at almost 90 degrees into an adjacent road. There was a beer tent halfway round and, having refreshed parts other things cannot reach, I played a good deal better on the second nine. It was a pleasant day, but the presence of Ian Botham and his wife led my thoughts back to the strain he must have been under at that point. To his great credit Guy didn't show any stress at all, but played his round with a constant smile, dealing with the hundreds of autograph hunters and mixing as sociably as ever in the bar afterwards. But I could not believe he felt particularly relaxed. I knew nothing of the alleged incident with Henry Blofeld at Bermuda other than what I had read, but it did strike me that Ian was doing himself no favours in his current precarious position. Sometimes his bullish temperament makes him his own worst enemy, and I wondered whether he might not kill himself off as England captain before anyone pulled the trigger on him.

The first representative match of any season is always MCC against the champion county, in 1981 Middlesex, and it is customary for the captain of the recently completed tour to lead an MCC side liberally sprinkled with players who promise some sort of Test future. On this occasion, however, Botham was unavailable because on the day the game began he was appearing in court to answer an assault charge. Surrey's Roger Knight captained a team which, rather to my surprise, included D.I. Gower and G.A. Gooch. I did not think we fell into the category of promising youngsters and could see little point in the exercise, although the occasion probably warrants the presence of some established Test players. Lulu made the most of his inclusion with a century. I failed twice, in a match played before almost empty stands and with very little atmosphere. As always, the county side treated it as a practice for more competitive events to come, and I have to say I had a struggle to remember the scores within only hours of the game finishing.

On Friday, the final day of the game, both Knight and I were due to play in a benefit match for Robin Jackman, under floodlights at Crystal Palace football club. As Jackers was also in the MCC side the operation was fraught with difficulties, and we eventually decided that the only way to beat the Friday evening traffic and get to the ground on time was by helicopter. It cost Jackers £300 for a ten-minute journey, and even then his worries were far from over. All afternoon, as the game at Lord's dragged towards a draw, Robin was on the phone to the Weather Centre, checking whether conditions were good enough for a landing. His concerned reports back to us grew steadily more hilarious as the departure time approached.

Finally it was decided that the flight could go ahead. The frantic dash began in a police squad car, which raced from St John's Wood to Battersea Heliport in twenty minutes – about half the time it would have taken any commuter driver – and deposited the three of us next to the helicopter. Having enjoyed my maiden flight in Guyana, I was quite looking forward to this panoramic view of rush-hour London, but I found it rather scary. This was a cramped four-seater which appeared to wobble spectacularly, and I didn't feel very safe. At times like this I am often reminded of childhood events, and I suddenly found myself thinking back to the day when my junior school had an outing to London and I ran all the way up the stairs of the Monument, reached the top and eagerly grabbed the railings for a view over the city – then felt dreadfully sick. Heights have never been my strong point. We landed safely on the pitch at Crystal Palace just as the teams were being presented, and although only 1500 people had turned up on a bitterly cold night, I think Jackers considered the effort had been worthwhile.

After the constant pace bowling in the West Indies it was fitting that my first Championship match of the season should be against Middlesex, whose new-ball bowlers were Wayne Daniel and Jeff Thomson. Tommo, in his first county game, was very quick, considering the slowness of the pitch, and in the murky light – so different from the brightness of the Caribbean – he was something of a handful.

I failed to get going in that game, so when we were badly beaten by Glamorgan in our opening Benson & Hedges zonal match, it had been a thoroughly bleak start to the season. That game against Glamorgan gave us our first experience of the new circles, thirty yards from the bat, and the regulation which allows only five men to stand outside them. It must be a good idea, because it makes the fielding captain think a lot more and renders negative tactics much more difficult. None of us played especially well against Glamorgan, but Ray East had a particularly unhappy day. He was out for nought, he did not bowl, and he once let the ball through his legs for four. That evening he related this sad saga on the phone to his Irish wife, Barbara, obviously expecting some sympathy. Instead he got the reply: 'So what are you doing down there?' He had no answer for that.

But then Essex beat Somerset in the Benson, and I made a century. The relief was great, because up to that game I had failed to pass 15 in five innings. I did not feel I was playing badly, yet I kept getting out. Perhaps it was a reaction after a difficult tour, but it was certainly frustrating. As things transpired, our existence in the Benson & Hedges competition hung on our final group match, against Kent at Dartford. Either we went through to the last eight, or they did. It was sudden death. We quietly fancied ourselves to win this one, but both Mike McEvoy and I were out quickly and unusually, caught down the leg-side – the kind of thing that normally only happens a couple of times a season. From 20 for three it was a long crawl back, and we didn't quite make it.

Not quite the end of May, and already Essex were out of one of the major competitions. We had lost some confidence and we were certainly not looking like the team which had played so powerfully in 1978 and 1979. Injuries to key men like Ken McEwan and Keith Fletcher had aggravated the position, and with Nobby Phillip not bowling too well John Lever lacked the strike bowler he needed as his partner with the new ball. We had, however, made an encouraging start in the John Player League, where I always believe a few wins breed a few more (though don't ask me why). Even more important, the famous Essex spirit was still remarkably high, and as usual the manic duo of East and Keith Pont figured largely in the fun.

Ray had a calf injury in the early weeks of the season, and although it did not stop him playing it did allow him to escape the trials of road running, which he particularly despises. On a number of rainy days at Chelmsford the rest of us set off in hoods and caps against the elements while Ray stayed in the warmth of the dressing-room, languidly doing a dozen step-ups on to the bench with his eyes riveted on the TV golf.

At Derby in early June Fletch was not fit enough to play, so Raymond took over the captaincy. But when Kenny McEwan was injured midway through the game Fletch came on as twelfth man and automatically began to direct operations. Umpire David Evans told him at lunchtime that this was against the regulations, so when we went out to field again Ray produced a long sheet of paper at the end of each over and pretended he was setting the field from Fletch's written instructions. Ponty began to emerge a few years ago as Ray's comic apprentice and is now a very amusing personality. This season he developed a new routine in his repertoire: every time he came off the field after batting he would adopt his idea of a military voice and give a speech from the front about 'what hell it was out there'. It was enough to earn him a new nickname, 'The General'.

The time was rapidly approaching for me to rejoin England, and in these days of six Tests per year, plus a series of one-day internationals, England regulars get to see very little of their county sides after the first part of June. I knew I was under pressure. It was a pleasant, tingling sort of pressure – the knowledge that I was expected to do well, because I had been successful on tour. England were being widely tipped to keep the Ashes with a comfortable win over the Australians – always a dangerous assumption – and it was perfectly obvious that the public were banking on plenty of runs from Geoff Boycott, David Gower and myself.

Unlike some sportsmen I freely admit that I do read the papers, and I am constantly aware of what is written about me. It often makes life more difficult – whether one is being built up as a hero or knocked down as a villain – but as this new series began I felt confident enough to cope. The nerves were there, but they did not dominate me. I believed we would win the one-day internationals and, with hindsight, still think we should have done. Instead, we lost two–one, and also lost a good deal of credibility and, inevitably, a psychological advantage. The one-day games are nowhere near as important to any player as the Tests, but they are watched by massive audiences, both live and on TV, and command considerable publicity. By coming out of them so poorly we had got ourselves into bad habits; the Australians had started their tour by winning, and I am sure they felt confident. No one likes losing any game, and although Ian Botham tried to shrug off the defeats as insignificant in the context of what was to come, I felt keenly that it was a very bad start to the summer. The one-day matches are easily described. We won the first convincingly; lost the second needlessly; and were outplayed in the third.

Victory in the opening contest at Lord's came so easily that defeat in the next was a major shock. It was that second game, at Edgbaston, which was critical. Ian Botham put Australia in, as he did on all three occasions, and they left us a target of 230. It should have been a lot less, but neither Peter Willey nor I bowled well and it was a tactical mess since I had to bowl at the end, when the slog was at its peak. Even so, the pitch was good and flat, and 230 in 55 overs should not have been beyond us. We lost our three senior players – Boycott, Gooch and Gower – all too quickly, but Mike Gatting and Jimmy Love had played us back into a winning position. We wanted 25 of the last five overs with five wickets left, and should have coasted in. But the captain was out to a bad shot, Gatt was out hitting and suddenly we were at panic stations. We lost three wickets in Dennis Lillee's final over, and the game had crazily slipped away from us. At Headingley, in the last game, we allowed them too many runs. The target was similar to that at Edgbaston, but twice as difficult in conditions ideal for seam and swing bowlers. We never looked like winning it.

So England had suffered another setback, and perhaps it was another nail in Ian Botham's captaincy coffin. He had kept the job to start the series, but only for the First Test, and there could scarcely have been a clearer indication that the selectors were considering a change of leader. On the eve of the First Test Bob Willis was widely quoted as saying that Ian should not do the job. Some newspapers construed the remarks – taken out of context from a local radio interview about his new book – as a direct attack by Bob on his captain. In fact, what Bob was doing was defending his long-time friend who, he believed, had been put in an intolerable position and was accordingly suffering as a player.

Bob was later fined a nominal amount by the TCCB for a technical breach of discipline, but like many others I agreed with what he said. Certainly, I felt it helped nobody to make Botham captain one match at a time. It was like making him walk a tightrope, one slip from disaster, and the edginess spread to every player in the squad. I should have thought he was either the right man for the job, so deserved a run of at least three Tests, or had by now been proved an ill-fitting choice and should have been replaced. The unpalatable possibility that the selectors could simply not make up their minds as to who should replace him was by now standard talk in every newspaper. Two names headed the list of contenders – Mike Brearley, aged thirty-nine, and Keith Fletcher, aged thirty-seven. Either, I felt, would do a good job in the current difficult position.

It is always more difficult to judge the merits of a captain at home than on tour. In England he just turns up the day before a Test and leads the team for five days, without the concerns of off-field policy and such great demands on man-management. And on the field, I will say, Ian had improved. His tactical sense seemed to have been sharpened by experience, but even so he was still not motivating players, and still not talking to the team in the inspirational manner I had grown used to under both Brearley and Fletcher.

10

Back to Brearley

*England went one down in the Ashes series after a dramatic First
Test on a widely condemned Trent Bridge pitch. Conjecture mounted
that Ian Botham would be sacked, but the selectors gave him a final
chance, perhaps more through the absence of an obvious successor
than because of any real faith that things would change. The Lord's
Test, traditionally the second of the series, began in dazzling
sunshine but was later punctuated by poor weather before reaching
an unexpectedly tense climax as Botham declared in mid-afternoon
on the final day in a last-ditch bid for glory. At the time, it seemed he
might be gambling all on a victory that would preserve his job. In
fact that was far from the case. By the time he arrived at headquarters on that last day, Tuesday, 7 July, Botham had already decided
that he would be resigning the captaincy at the end of the match.*

It was a shock to almost all of us. We were winding down
in the cavernous home dressing-room at Lord's, which
always wears a slightly untidy look but never loses its
special atmosphere. Ian had walked out of the room without a word to us; it transpired he had gone to find Alec
Bedser. When he came back, he called for attention and
quietly announced that he would be standing down from
the captaincy because he believed the current match-to-
match basis was harming the team's morale, quite apart
from his own. Reaction was muted. There were some
mutterings of sympathy, one or two surprised noises –
because few of us had expected the change to be made in
this manner – but generally an air of relief that the issue had
been dragged into the open and settled by Ian himself.

I later learned that he had discussed the problem at length with his wife, Kathy, at the team's hotel the previous evening. Kathy had probably suffered the pressures more than Ian, and had certainly become sensitive about all the criticism he was taking. Ian himself could have borne it, I imagine, but perhaps the decision was partly made to protect his family from further stress. Whatever his reasons, I admired him for having the courage to take the matter out of the selectors' hands. Scarcely a day had passed in the preceding weeks without a newspaper or media commentator speculating on the next captain, and with only the tenuous security of one match at a time Ian must have felt his authority hopelessly undermined. The situation had not been good for the team, either. Spirit had been shaky since the Caribbean tour, the Trent Bridge defeat had dented it further, and the leadership issue was a constant, unsettling irritant to players who knew that a change of captain could lead to a change of policy and the loss of their job.

I felt sorry for Ian. We have not always seen eye-to-eye on cricket matters, and our lifestyles do not coincide. But despite this lack of any real affinity I respect his immense cricket ability and did not want to see it being eroded any further by responsibilities which, in my opinion, were having adverse effects on him. Right to the end, and even after his resignation, Ian insisted that his form had never suffered through the captaincy. Perhaps he felt he had to say that, firstly to retain the job and later to keep any hope of getting it back; or perhaps he had really convinced himself that it was so. Personally, I felt the captaincy had worn away some of his brilliant flair, and I was glad he had got out in time to put things right.

As a final kick in the teeth, Alec Bedser admitted at a press conference that same evening that Ian would have been sacked in any case, and that a replacement had already been decided upon. I wondered whether this was a necessary admission. Surely Ian should have been allowed to go quietly, with some pride left? His recent life had been one long complicated chain of problems, on and off the field, and if only half of them were influenced by the captaincy he was right to go. No job is worth that much. Ian went off to Taunton, to play in a Benson & Hedges Cup semi-final and receive a hero's welcome from his home crowd. It is an odd but perennial fact that, as long as you are failing in a job, you are a villain. As soon as you admit that failure by resigning, you become a hero. Maybe Ian never would admit he had failed – I have never heard him talk that way about anything. He is one of the world's greatest optimists, and I am quite sure he went away from Lord's that night believing that he would be back again as captain.

I thought it unlikely, and did not base my judgement on the widely quoted statistic that he had led England in twelve Tests without achieving one victory. The critics were forever pointing out that this was the worst record of any England skipper, but perhaps they missed the point that nine of those Tests had been against the West Indies, one of the strongest teams ever to play international cricket. I don't think any other captain could have changed the result of those two series, but I do believe the team could have been better led, and gone out feeling more psyched-up. Right to the very end, Ian never quite learned the art which Mike Brearley perfects, of making individuals feel good in themselves and also part of a motivated unit who expect to win. Captains can be either born or made. I don't think Ian was a born skipper, and nobody had given him the chance to make himself one. It was all thrust upon him too soon – and a series against the ruthless West Indians is no place for quietly learning the niceties of your job.

He had again taken some criticism in the First Test at Trent Bridge, and I must say I was surprised that he survived it to lead us again at Lord's. It was a bad defeat, on the type of pitch traditionally expected to suit English bowlers. Ron Allsop, the groundsman, had been preparing fast, grassy pitches for Notts and, although he cut the Test strip a little shorter, it was plain at a glance that, as in the previous year's Test there against the West Indies, the batsmen were due for a hard time. Both teams picked four seamers, and naturally we believed that our quartet – Willis, Dilley, Botham and Hendrick – could exploit the conditions more effectively than theirs, and that we would probably win a low-scoring game. We were right about the low scores, but underestimated their bowlers; we lost the game on catching, something at which England sides of recent years have been so outstanding. How can you explain why a team which has fielded and caught safely for some years should suddenly develop such a spectacular attack of butterfingers? It was just just the odd one or two catches that were dropped; it was more like half a dozen, and the disease spread through the side.

We had batted first and made 185. Kim Hughes put us in, which was to be expected, and Geoff Boycott and I received swift confirmation that the groundsman's praiseworthy efforts to produce more pace and bounce had also given the seamers the opportunity to move the ball laterally off the seam. Terry Alderman was to most of us an unknown quantity. He used to be a tearaway, we were told, but was now very much like a typical English seamer; certainly that was true – and a good one, too. He used the conditions to great advantage, bowling at modest pace but nipping the ball either way off the pitch, and no one played him with comfort. I was out cheaply to Lillee. For some reason, I was not as confident as I had been at a similar stage in 1980. It was difficult to explain why. I had been successful on tour, which was after all not so long before, but I felt out of touch, in need of a long innings to regain confidence. Trent Bridge was never likely to give me that chance.

We had agreed that 200 would be a good score, potentially a winning one, so our final total was anything but disastrous. It should, indeed, have been enough, because if we had held on to those catches Australia would not have made many more than 100. Instead, Allan Border batted on to a half-century which was decisive in the context of the game, yet he had twice been reprieved by our generosity.

114

Good catchers do not suddenly become bad overnight, but I believe that one good catch can breed another – in other words, confidence spreads through a team once one or two players have held on to difficult chances. But if it goes the other way and you drop everything, not a great deal can be done. Certainly you can practise, but as a Test team we have always done that as a matter of routine. However many times you may catch the ball as it is hit to you in the outfield before play, you have no guarantee of taking the one which comes at you during the match itself. The one chance which came my way went down, and because it was the only catch offered to me I thought back over recent months and recalled that I had stood at slip throughout four Tests in the Caribbean, taking one catch and dropping another. Although it does not amount to an excuse, it did seem unusual that five Tests had only brought three chances. I had lost some confidence in my ability at slip, and felt I would profit from moving else-where, but after the Nottingham experience I knew I was not the only player to feel that way.

Australia reached 179, only six runs behind, and the pitch was still showing no indication of weakening its grip. I had concluded that, however long you fought it out, the pitch would get you eventually, so I began my second innings with the intention of attacking anything wide or short. It did not make me many runs, but I still believe it was the correct theory in the circumstances.

We were bowled out early on the fourth day, which was a Sunday for the first time ever in an English Test. We had experimentally sacrificed the rest day, which is not essen-tial in the cool English climate; I am very much in favour of play on Sundays if it can be justified by bigger atten-dances, as it was in this instance. Television, however, is a different and delicate matter, and a conflict has clearly arisen with the interest of the counties' Sunday competi-tion, the John Player League. BBC proposed to televise John Player games only when Tests were not being played, and this seemed wrong. My view is that the Sun-days of Tests should never be televised, because it tempts people away from the county games, where the Sunday crowds have recently done so much to keep counties' finances buoyant.

The live and television audiences on this revolutionary Sunday certainly had value for money. We had managed only 125, a poor score but still only about 50 short of a winning position. As it was, we bowled pretty well and gave the Australians a few moments of panic. But, as if on cue, the weather had improved and the sun had taken much of the devil out of the wicket. Although Graham Dilley took four wickets in a late, despairing spell, we were beaten by a further four.

So while the Australians' dressing-room resounded to deafening songs and chants, ours was subdued and deflated. Ian was told by Alec Bedser that he was being given another Test, and while the press speculated on whether the selectors had tried to persuade Mike Brearley back for a year, we went off to our various county commitments. Morale was at its lowest ebb in all the time I had been associated with the England side. Luck, I always think, runs for winners. Success breeds more success. England were enjoying very few good breaks, and the spirit of the side was naturally suffering.

The Australians, quite rightly, were euphoric about the victory. They had come to England with very little hope, according to their own media; I had therefore been rather startled when the phone next to my bed in Nottingham's Albany Hotel rang on the first morning of the Test, and an Aussie voice informed me that I was about to be transmitted live to a South Australian audience and would I give my views on the coming series? I told him to phone back. After I had woken myself up I agreed to do the interview, the innocent tone of which was captured by the first question – is it raining there? Snap interviews across the world are commonplace on Australian radio, I'm told, and this one at least reassured me that Kim Hughes' side had not been prematurely dumped by their country. After Nottingham, there was no chance of that.

One great problem with Test cricket these days is that it

allows for so few three-day county games. The Nottingham Test finished on the Sunday, which meant I had to sit
out the next two days while Essex were trounced by
Sussex at Ilford. The Wednesday, as is unfortunately the
habit now, was devoted to a cup round in which Essex
were not involved. So between Tests I had one first-class
match in which to repair my confidence with a big score.
It was clearly not enough, so I asked Keith Fletcher if
there was a second-team match I could play. Happily,
they had arranged a two-day fixture on the Thursday and
Friday against a team called the Willows, surreptitiously
on tour from South Africa. I not only played, but captained the side. Second-team cricket can work two ways: it
can either provide a boost to confidence, or help to destroy
it completely. For me, after batting fifteen minutes in two
innings at Nottingham, this match did nothing but harm.
I scored 12 before being bowled, and sat for the next two
hours watching Alan Lilley score 120.

What I needed was a hard, flat wicket and a three-day
match: Leicester provided the perfect answer. I scored
162 there on the Saturday, despite having a brainstorm on
96. I was aiming to reach 100 before lunch and miss-hit the
left-arm spinner Nick Cook to mid-on, but Les Taylor
seemed to have caught the England bug and the catch
went down. The runs made me feel a great deal better,
even though the pitch was as different as possible from the
track half an hour up the M1 at Nottingham. David
Gower, another who had failed in the Test, scored 156 not
out on the second day, and I made 87 in the second
innings. At one stage, 950 runs had been scored for the fall
of six wickets, yet we still got close to winning it on the
final evening. Leicester finished seven wickets down, and
the knowledge that we might well have won if a few more
catches had stuck seemed ironically familiar.

Only one change had been made to the squad for the
Second Test, and that was in the wicketkeeping position.
Paul Downton had dropped a catch at Trent Bridge and,
while he was far from alone in that, it was a simple and
ultimately vital chance given by Border. The selectors

117

opted to recall the experienced Bob Taylor. I was delighted to welcome back the fellow we all call Chat, but it left me pondering the inconsistencies of it all. Including one-day internationals, England had now made eight wicketkeeping changes in not much more than twelve months. In my view injustice had been done to both Alan Knott and Taylor himself. I could not understand why Bob had not been recalled as soon as the selectors had decided that Knott should be left out – and it would need very forceful logic to persuade me that his omission from the winter tour was fair.

The man left out on the morning of the game was Mike Hendrick. Thought by many to be the best seam bowler in England, Hendo has consistently failed to produce the figures to justify his ranking. He has never, for instance, taken five wickets in an innings for England. While he often seems an unlucky bowler, you cannot get away with that for ever. The time comes when people look for other reasons for your lack of success, and in Mike's case I believe it is because he bowls to a constant length, which on poor wickets is a fraction too short. He always bowls the same way, but this lack of adjustment does mean that he cuts down his options. By the same token, he can seldom pick up any l.b.w.s. He will beat the bat by a long way, which prompts people to call him unlucky. But in certain circumstances, fine bowler that he is, Mike becomes more a negative instrument than a positive weapon.

The team met, as always, on the Wednesday afternoon before the Test. Even at home we have an informal team dinner on the eve of each Test, but as I live only twenty miles from Lord's I prefer to go home each night rather than use a hotel. The sun was shining, there was a fine crowd, the pitch looked good and we were put in to bat. I felt very good for an hour, but after making 44 I misjudged a pull to be caught at square leg. It was a dreadful feeling, much worse than being out for nought, because I had been there long enough to start commanding the bowlers, and it is always a sin to get out then.

As Tests go, this was no classic. Draw was written all over it from a very early stage, but Lord's, as ever, gave me a very special feeling: it could just be the large crowd, but I think the ground has a hold over me that no other cricket venue can rival. I have often done well there in big matches, when the wickets are normally good and the boundaries passably short; I find the atmosphere quite unique, both inside the historic pavilion and on the playing area itself.

The pitch certainly wore quite noticeably, and our gamble on the last day, when we scored quick runs and declared soon after lunch, was a worthwhile long shot. It was never very likely that England could win, but there was certainly no chance of the Australians making the runs. John Emburey was our likely key bowler, but although I felt he bowled reasonably well he failed to take a wicket, so our challenge petered out. In any case, the match itself was forgotten within minutes of the end. Ian Botham's resignation, or sacking, demanded the attention of all the media. When I got home I sat in the garden, wondering whether the new captain would be Brearley or Fletcher . . . I could not imagine that any other candidate could have been seriously considered. Just before ten, the phone rang: Mike Brearley speaking. The decision had been made.

11

Misery amid the Miracles

Like all those before him who have had the dubious privilege of taking on the captaincy of a losing team, Mike Brearley was hailed as a potential saviour by some, while his appointment was seen as retrograde by others. He continued to stress that he was unavailable for the winter tour to India, but emphasized that his enthusiasm for Test cricket remained and that he regarded as a new and exciting challenge his return to the job he had left barely a year earlier. Not even Brearley, for all his intellectual shrewdness, could have forecast just how exciting it was going to be.

When you have been out twice in a day without scoring a run, when your team has followed on and when the hotel receptionist has asked if you would like to check out on the fourth morning of the match, you do not expect to win. But, just occasionally in cricket the miraculous occurs.

The Leeds Test was a spectacular series of contradictions. It had begun with two days of pedestrian cricket that looked certain to lead to a draw. But there followed a hectic England collapse which seemed equally certain to end in defeat, probably by an innings. Then, suddenly, the match was turned on its head by an outrageous century from Ian Botham, performing like someone who had just rediscovered his Superman outfit after a year of vain searching. The whole, crazy mix was topped up by a superb spell of bowling by Bob Willis. You could say Ian saved the match and Bob won it, his eight for 43 being the best figures of a career which Bob himself confessed he had thought finished when he flew back from the Caribbean.

We won by 18 runs. It was an emotional, almost hysterical last day. The facts were impossible to take in. Afterwards, on the players' balcony at Headingley, we all just looked at each other, grinning and muttering inane words of congratulation, but not quite believing what had happened. It was the most extraordinary Test I have played in, and yet if you take out the final day and the incredible result it was also the most deflating.

The adage that you are only as good as your last performance has some truth in it. I could not go on relying on my reputation. My success in the West Indies was beginning to seem unpleasantly distant, and these two failures at Leeds had got through to me. For some days I felt unusually depressed about my form and future. It was not that I doubted my ability, for I had proved several times that I could make runs at the highest level of the game, and nobody can become a bad player overnight. Nor did I feel I was necessarily playing badly, because a brisk 100 in the John Player League match on the Sunday after the Leeds Test meant I had scored centuries in each of the four major county competitions during the season – something nobody else had managed.

The theory was being bandied around that I was suspect against the moving ball, but I did not accept that. In England, you are always batting against movement in the air and off the seam; it was not something I was encountering for the first time. To my mind, the plain truth was that I was going through the type of bad spell that afflicts every Test match player at some stage. The possibility that in the past few years I had played too much top-level cricket, with all its attendant pressures, was something that preyed on my mind, and I kept wondering if I needed a break. After Leeds I did not expect to play in the next Test, and I was not sure whether it might be better if I was left out, just to rest and regain confidence in my ability.

These were the morbid thoughts I took away from a Test which none of us is ever likely to forget, least of all Mike Brearley, whose winning knack as skipper had clearly not deserted him even in such daunting adversity.

121

I have said before that I considered Brearley and Keith Fletcher the best captains in English cricket, and one of the qualities they both possess is the ability to command respect from all players. The England side was unanimous in its genuine welcome for Brearley and a feeling that, if anybody could stem the dismal tide in which we were caught up, it was Mike.

Mike can gather in his players and make them feel a team; he can motivate without shouting; and he can tap and boost individual players' morale without pandering to them. This situation was to be a particular trial for him since he had seen little of the previous two Tests and had not been to the Caribbean. So when we met as usual on the afternoon before the game the discussions were fuller than usual. We talked through the relative strengths of the opposition, chatted over the things we had been doing wrong, and assessed how best to put them right. One of the main points of conversation once again was slip catching, and Mike decided that we should switch the positions occasionally, so that the five or six people who could field in the slip area took turns.

Chris Old was back for this match; it was his first involvement with the side since his unhappy and unprofitable tour. Chilly always seems a far more effective bowler in English conditions, and since his home patch at Leeds was particularly likely to suit his bowling this was very much a horses-for-courses selection. If that caused a minor stir, the omission of John Emburey on the morning of the game produced a major one. He was the only specialist spinner in the twelve, and as local pre-match forecasts had suggested some turn later in the game it was a decision which surprised a great many people, probably including Embers himself.

By the end of that day the ball appeared to have moved little for the seamers and Australia were past 200 with only three wickets down, having chosen to bat when our selection had probably committed us to put them in anyway. Mike approached John and apologized, admitting that he now thought he had made a mistake. But in fact later events suggested that his original decision was justified. Kim Hughes had not immediately opted to bat when he won the toss for the third time in succession. He had gone so far as to return to the middle some minutes later, with his vice-captain Rod Marsh, and once more study the pitch before making up his mind. It was obviously a difficult choice, since by tradition Headingley favours the bowlers on the first morning, affording more bounce and movement off the wicket than on the following days. This time, however, England failed to exploit the advantage, John Dyson kept his head down for most of the day to make a gritty century, and we were clearly under the cosh.

We did not feel that our bowlers had performed badly – although on reflection they bowled too wide – but yet again our catching and our luck were poor. Four chances went down, including another slip chance to me, and any amount of nicks and edges failed to carry to hand. It was a frustrating day, and Friday was little better. Kim Hughes and Graham Yallop both passed 50, and Australia amassed 401 before declaring, to leave us ten minutes of batting in the evening gloom.

There was no reason for me to lack confidence. My most recent innings had been a century in the NatWest Trophy, on a club wicket at Hitchin where Hertfordshire's experienced new-ball bowler was making leg-cutters perform contortions at a very respectable pace. We had won, gaining revenge for a humiliating defeat on the same ground five years earlier, and the runs should have done me no harm. But it wasn't quite a Test match. . . . I survived the short evening session, although Terry Alderman bowled me a delivery which pitched on middle and leg and took off at such an angle that Marsh had to leap across in front of first slip to hold it.

That night we were invited to a dinner given by Ladbroke's, the bookmakers, in the casino restaurant which adjoins the Dragonara Hotel, our base for every Leeds Test. Among the guests were Ron Pollard and Godfrey Evans, between them responsible for setting the company's cricket odds. They told us some fascinating tales of strange bets, including one request from an American lady who wanted to wager 25 dollars on an alien landing on earth, dead or alive, before the end of the year. Ladbroke's gave her odds of 500–1. We were to remember that story rather vividly twenty-four hours later, for at the end of the third day's play we were following on, I was already out in the second innings, and Messrs Evans and Pollard were offering those same odds of 500–1 against England!

The first ball I had faced that day was straight and full. I played across the line, missed, and had no complaints about being given out l.b.w. It was not the type of ball anyone relishes first up, but neither was it the type of shot I care to remember. There are two distinct methods of being dismissed in cricket. You are either out playing an authentic stroke to a ball which is simply too good for you, or you are out playing a poor stroke. The one consoling factor for the England team on this horrible day was that 10 of the 12 wickets to fall were the results of very good deliveries.

Ian Botham got one of the most brutal balls of all, but he had already added a half-century to the six wickets he had taken in the Australian innings. Mike had told him just to go out and bat in his natural fashion – something he had not always done as captain. He hit straight and well, clearly enjoying the freedom. But whether he was enjoying not being captain was something he was not prepared to admit. Pressed by the media for a reason for his return of form, he would only refer to his own Catch-22 situation – if he confessed he was playing better without the captaincy, he could not hope to regain it.

We were all out 227 runs behind, the other main feature of the innings being the catch which brought Rodney Marsh to a new Test record. Since I have been playing at Test level Marsh has always impressed me. Standing back he is acrobatic and secure, perhaps the best in the world. Standing up for the spinners, he has improved immeasurably in recent years – and this despite having such limited practice, as the Australian team have been dominated by seam. He has gained a reputation for being a hard character on the field, not averse to handing out some verbal abuse to opposing batsmen, but I have experienced this very rarely. Off the field he is generally a delightful man, friendly and sociable.

The light was fading when I faced up to the follow-on, and I survived only two balls before pushing forward and nicking the third to slip. It was the first time I had ever been out twice in a day in Test cricket, let alone without scoring, and my depression turned to irritation when the umpires immediately conferred and brought the players off for bad light before another ball had been bowled. There was no question of the light having deteriorated since the start of the over, so I had been dismissed in unfit conditions. It does not constitute a personal excuse, but I do think it a very unfair inconsistency in the game, and since it happened twice to David Gower in the West Indies I now know how he felt.

After another brief session, in which we managed to avoid further disasters, the light grew too bad again. The umpires inspected once more at five to six, knowing that the rules stated that conditions had to be fit at six if the extra hour was to be allowed. Two minutes before six, with a dark cloud overhead, they abandoned play for the day. Something like three minutes later, the sun was beating down. Not surprisingly, the crowd was unhappy. Something similar had occurred during the Lord's Test, and the public reaction was the same – they hurled hundreds of cushions on to the playing area and chanted anti-umpire slogans. A group of spectators gathered in front of the pavilion, some demanding their money back, others just calling for an explanation. Umpire Barry Meyer tried to give one, but his voice was drowned by the noise. In my view, the umpires acted within the regulations on this occasion; but the rule was clearly a silly one, and the TCCB moved quickly to amend it so that the extra hour would come into operation whether or not play was possible at the scheduled finishing time.

Saturday night was spent at a barbecue at Ian Botham's house; on Sunday I was with my old friend Phil Carrick of Yorkshire at another barbecue. Both were convivial occasions, but I still felt low-spirited when I arrived at the ground on Monday morning. The pitch was now showing its true colours, which reflected poorly on our first-innings bowling performance after all, and few of us held out much hope for surviving beyond this fourth day. Ian Botham had gone so far as to check out of the hotel, but if he was cheekily tempting fate he was very soon directing it in his own inimitable way.

We were 105 for five when Botham went in to bat. That became 135 for seven shortly before tea, and by all logic the game seemed sure of completion before the close of play. Guy knew there was nothing to lose, and such do-or-die situations are absolutely made for him. After a cursory look at the pitch and the bowling, he proceeded to try and hit every ball for four. At a guess, he was succeeding four times out of six. You can make allowance for someone batting like that and scoring 50 or 60. In the context of this match that would have made no difference – we would still have been beaten by an innings. But to score 149 not out, as Ian did, had all the improbable charm of a story about Roy of the Rovers – which, incidentally, became Botham's new nickname.

One of the most remarkable things was that we were 130 ahead before he ran out of partners. Graham Dilley stayed eighty minutes and contributed almost half of an eighth-wicket stand worth 117; then Chris Old made 29 as the ninth wicket added 67 in fifty-five minutes. Even the last wicket yielded 37. The Australians, from being on the very brink of victory, gradually realized that a lot of work lay ahead. Their bowling lost its accuracy and the fielding became steadily more ragged. What is more, the bottles of champagne on ice in their dressing-room bath had to stay untouched. Unlike Guy's, their tempting of fate had been a disaster.

For all the magic of that innings, it still promised no more than a delay of the inevitable, for who would have thought that Bob 'Goose' Willis would bowl the Australian out in such dramatic style? At 56 for one, they had been going comfortably; we thought we might nip out another two or three of them, but that the end result would be like the depressing defeat we suffered at Trent Bridge and that we could see the Ashes slipping agonizingly away. It was then that Goose changed ends, to bowl downwind with the slope in his favour. Quite suddenly he began to rush in like a man possessed. He hit the right spot on the pitch and got the odd ball to rear alarmingly. Chappell, Hughes and Yallop were out to him in the space of two overs, while at the other end Chris Old took the vital wicket of Allan Border for nought. At 65 for five the odds had incredibly swung in our favour, and when Marsh and the dogged Dyson were both out to Bob victory was within reach.

The atmosphere out there was electric. Everybody was on their toes, the confidence was back and the catches were sticking. Mike was orchestrating it all with a cool composure few could have matched, while Bob charged up and down looking demented, his eyes wide and staring as if his mind was somewhere else entirely. Along with most of the other lads, I ran up to him now and again to say, 'Well bowled,' or to give a word of encouragement. But he either didn't hear or took no notice, for he marched back to his mark without once turning his head sideways to acknowledge the presence of anyone or anything else. When he is in such a situation Bob becomes so engrossed in his bowling, so carried away by the desire to win, that it is impossible to communicate with him. He takes time to wind down afterwards too, but no one minded that. When it was over, a yorker knocking out Ray Bright's middle stump, I remember chasing after him to slap him on the back; but I could not get close enough. He had wheeled once, arms raised aloft in a victory salute, and then sprinted for the dressing-room without a backward glance.

No adjectives could describe the victory, although the press tried manfully to find them. For us, as a team, it was gratifying to come back and win when everyone had written us off without mercy; although, if we were honest, not one of us would have thought there was a chance of avoiding defeat in mid-afternoon on the Monday.

127

12

The Impossible Is Commonplace

As if the Houdini escape at Headingley was not enough, England won again at Edgbaston in a fashion almost equally far-fetched. Again, the rejuvenated Botham was the match-winner; again, the recalled Brearley inspired his side as few other captains could have done. The first Sunday crowd for a Birmingham Test celebrated with Union Jacks and sang 'Rule Britannia', and suddenly everyone in the country appeared to be fascinated by a Test series which could so easily have been emphatically decided in Australia's favour. But victory still could not mask the shortcomings of England's batting form, and Gooch's place remained only tentatively intact.

Kim Hughes danced on a table in the Albany Hotel ballroom on the night of Sunday, 2 August, and Dennis Lillee led a chorus of singing. They were not celebrating so much as trying to forget that the impossible had happened for the second time in a fortnight. Instead of being three-nil ahead with the Ashes won, as they might so easily have been, Hughes' side were two–one down and, in the words of that old song, bewitched, bothered and bewildered. Quite by coincidence, a ball had been arranged for that night in the hotel where the Australians were staying. It was for Bob Willis' benefit, and the players of both teams were invited. Only two of the Australians lingered after the formal part – captain and star bowler – and if the departure of the rest was disappointing, it was also understandable. I know how I would have felt in their position.

In a way, this result had been still less conceivable than

the victory at Leeds, because while the Headingley pitch was constantly unpleasant to bat on, Edgbaston's wicket was no worse than slightly uneven. Yet Australia, needing only 150 on the fourth day for a win which seemed a formality, were dismissed 29 runs short. It was, of course, marvellous stuff for the English game. Cricket was promoted overnight to front-page news. People in the street, who might not normally cross the road to watch a Test match, were earnestly and enthusiastically discussing this latest sensation. My only regret was that my personal contribution to the triumphs continued to be minor. At Edgbaston I made 21 in each innings, and once more expected to be dropped.

If you hit a bad patch as a batsman, it is often dreadfully difficult to halt the snowball effect. Each time you bat, one mistake is your last. If you are in good form, it seems natural to be given a life or two, to enjoy a little luck on the way. But when things are going wrong, even the breaks desert you. I was suffering that syndrome now and found it hard to explain. I was still making runs for Essex, after all, yet a look at my diary was revealing. I had played only seven Championship innings during the season, and was averaging 60. My last match was at the end of June; my next would be in the last week of August. Each time a Test finished I had a one-day cup match to play, probably followed by a John Player League game, a few idle days and another Test. It was no sort of preparation. I found the pressure was building on me in each Test innings, and if you cannot go out feeling confident of making runs – as I had felt only a few months earlier – the battle is well on the way to being lost.

Mike Brearley had asked me after the Leeds Test if I would object to batting number four. I replied that I did not mind, because batting anywhere for England is better than nowhere at all. On the Sunday before the Birmingham Test I saw on television that the change in order had been implemented. I dropped down to four, and Mike would open with Boycott. The number three position, which had caused problems since the start of the West

Indies tour, had passed to David Gower, something I could not agree with. David is a stroke player, who at Test level should not have to be subjected to the new ball. It is right that he should bat early for his county, because that is the only chance he has of building an innings, but at Test level I feel number four or five are his best positions.

Positional changes apart, the squad was unaltered from Leeds. Probably the selectors had planned something different, but that crazy final twenty-four hours at Headingley had left them with little choice. However, one change was eventually forced upon them by an injury to Graham Dilley. John Emburey returned, as he would surely have done anyway, so the disruption was negligible.

After the poor pitches at Nottingham and Leeds, we gathered at Edgbaston on the eve of the game expecting to see the usual good, flat wicket with very little grass. We were not disappointed – it looked just like most other Birmingham pitches and, indeed, played perfectly respectably throughout. Instead of the stereotyped, motel-style place in which we are so often housed for Tests, we stayed this time in some splendour at the Plough and Harrow. It stands just a few minutes from the ground and is a converted old inn, grandly furnished and elegant in every way. It was pleasantly different, and I am sure it was good for the players to be staying in such a relaxing environment. I can seldom sleep properly in hotels anywhere, but this one gave me a better chance than most.

The team meeting that night went over familiar ground. Naturally the batting remained our greatest concern, and I repeated my conviction that anyone who gets to 30 or 40 should make it count and not give themselves away as so many of us had been guilty of doing. Amazingly, at this point in the series there had been only two centuries, and of these only John Dyson's at Leeds was in any way orthodox. We wanted to win the toss and bat, and saw no real obstacles to scoring 300-plus on this pitch.

We did win the toss and bat, but that was where the success of the scheme ended. We were dismissed for 189, Alderman taking five for 42. What was worse, there could be no excuses this time. Most of us had simply played poor shots, and the depression which descended on the dressing-room that afternoon told the story more vividly than any words. I found myself feeling more nervous than usual before an innings. It was the first time in a long while that I had sat in the dressing-room with my pads on for any period. I became fidgety and tense. I did not think batting at number four was doing me much good. But when I got out there, I began to feel confident. I was striking the ball well enough, and had got past 20 when I let myself down with an ugly stroke at a short ball from Ray Bright. Rod Marsh took the catch and I just stood for a moment or two with my head thrown back in despair. Some people apparently thought I was unhappy to be given out, but that was not so. I was just upset with myself.

It is a well-worn excuse, I know, but I cannot help feeling that our troubles, mine included, were at least partly the result of playing too much one-day cricket and too few three-day games. In limited-over matches, it is easy for players to condition themselves to improvising. With no slips, you can run the ball down to third man with impunity. Try it in a Test, and eight times out of ten you will be caught.

Our mood was lightened a little towards the end of the day when Chris Old struck twice, and Australia finished a little rocky themselves at 13 for two. The second day was even, absorbing, and at times heated. Australia inched ahead by 69 runs, thanks mainly to Hughes and Martin Kent, who made 46 in his first Test innings. Yet the cricket was for a period so fiercely competitive that a number of people in the packed crowd cannot have known quite what was happening. It began during a furious spell from Willis. The batsmen were Hughes, who was relishing the challenge, and Graham Yallop, who apparently was not. Bob had disturbed Yallop with a couple of short balls, and Hughes took it upon himself to begin refusing long singles, in order to keep Yallop away from the strike. To me, this was not only undermining the confidence of one of his senior batsmen, but giving the bowler and fielders a psychological boost. I would not have liked it had I been in Yallop's position.

The effect on Willis was to make him bowl faster and faster. Roared on by a large group of chanting cheer-leaders, he stormed in at great speed and for half an hour or more we had electrifying cricket. Hughes got himself very worked up, frequently swearing loudly at himself and once or twice ironically applauding Goose for another short ball. The one man who did not seem to be enjoying the contest at all was umpire Dickie Bird, who fussed around in his usual fashion and only succeeded in aggravating things, when there was in fact very little niggle among the players themselves.

Later in that same session, however, Dennis Lillee arrived to bat and things happened even more swiftly. First, in the heat of the moment, he appeared to drop his shoulder and charge into Willis in the course of a run. Lillee raised his arm in immediate apology, but Bob stalked off in a great rage. Dickie Bird was three feet away and distraught! Then, when Lillee was facing the spin of Emburey with several men crowding round the bat, he pushed forward and the ball looped off his pad to Mike Gatting at short leg. Instinctively, I shouted from silly point, 'Catch it,' at which Lillee turned on me angrily and aimed an oath into my face. I retorted that I was only copying the Australian habit of appealing for anything. Bob Taylor intervened in his best diplomatic manner, telling us both to calm down, and he in turn was promptly rounded on by Lillee. It was all over very quickly, and any remaining acrimony was rapidly patched up at the close of play, but it did stress to me that Dennis is the type of cricketer who benefits from getting himself psyched up and in an aggressive mood.

We were only 20 runs behind by the close, with the captain out, and we set off on the Saturday morning with the intention of applying ourselves studiously. Our determination to hang on to wickets, as we failed to do in the first innings, was obvious by the slow rate of scoring –

only 21 scoring strokes were played in 32 overs up to lunch. But the policy was not an overwhelming success: although four of our top five batsmen passed 20, not one of them reached 40. Boycott took some heavy criticism the following day for his painstaking progress to 29. He seemed to me to be playing in the same vein as ever, and if his slowness was exaggerated by the state of the game, I do not really subscribe to the view that he has a bad influence on more junior batsmen.

For the second time in the match I got out to Bright at 21, this time bowled as I went to hit him straight. He had bowled flat and tightly on a length from over the wicket, but I just could not see him bowling us out. Once more, however, I made one miscalculation and paid for it, walking off resigned to the fact that I would not be required again at Test level for a while now. From the depths of 116 for six we somehow reached 219. Chris Old was promoted to swing the bat against Bright, and it worked. Then John Emburey shared valuable stands with Mike Gatting and Bob Taylor. He finished with 37 not out, but who could have thought that night, when Australia lost a quick wicket to Old again, that those runs would be the difference between the expected defeat and another astonishing win?

Sunday was brilliantly hot and sunny and another huge crowd arrived. Perhaps they were expecting another miracle, but most of us felt that lightning could not strike twice. Significantly, as we sat in the luxurious lounge of the Plough and Harrow after breakfast that morning, Ian Botham was full of bravado. He had no doubts we would win again, he said, but could not decide by how many runs. Roy of the Rovers was loving his new role, but his joking boasts were not going to prove as ridiculous as they sounded.

Australia only needed another 142, and the pitch was still good. Surely they could not fail? Eventually they did fail because, I believe, they were recalling the disaster at Headingley. Quite simply, they panicked under pressure. Willis had made the first incisions with two wickets in the morning, but soon after lunch they had reached 87 for three. Yallop and Allan Border had put on 58 and, even though Emburey had bowled his off-spin well, the match seemed to be slipping away. Our comfort at that stage was that we were not sacrificing it without a fight. But suddenly Yallop was out to Emburey, a catch at silly point by Botham. And then came the ball which really turned the game. It was the perfect delivery from Emburey, turning and lifting alarmingly. Border could not keep it down, and it was 105 for five. I knew then that we had a chance; the feeling was strong because we had proved once before that it could be done.

Brearley brought a crowd of men up around the bat, then recalled Roy of the Rovers, and the game was over. Ian said later he had not wanted to bowl, because he thought others had a better chance than himself. But once he had the ball in his hand he steamed in as I had not seen him do for months, bowling straight, fast and to a full length. In twenty-eight deliveries he took five wickets for one run, and Australia were all out for 121. Australia had only needed one man to make a score, but nobody did. It was not until later that I realized the entire Test had been played on a largely blameless pitch without a single half-century. That was the most amazing statistic of all.

As for Botham, man of the match again, it was great to see his confidence flowering. The captaincy, more clearly than ever, was a burden he did not need – what he did need was Mike bringing out the best in him. I don't know what the chemistry is between them, except that it relies greatly on mutual mickey-taking and an underlying respect; but it works. When Ian plays well the team thrives, and in two Tests – for all the heroics of Bob Willis – Botham had been the difference between the sides.

13

Ashes and Apartheid

South Africa, who had been outlawed in international cricket since 1970, once again received little encouragement from the annual meeting of the International Cricket Conference in late July. Their response was swift. Promoters vied, sponsors hovered; many of the world's best and most famous players were approached about their interest in an unofficial 'Test' series in South Africa during the British winter of 1981–2. The sums of money involved were said to be immense. British newspapers seized on the story, and on 9 August it was revealed that a number of England players were among those who had been approached, and that a Test selector, John Edrich, was recruiting on behalf of a potential promoter.

The news about John Edrich came as a complete shock to me, though the possible involvement of England players did not. Six months earlier, while on tour in the Caribbean, I had been sounded out about an autumn series in South Africa, probably over a six-week period before the scheduled tour to India. The approach came from a businessman in South Africa, and the idea apparently was that either a full side of English Test players, or a strong World XI, would play against the best South Africa could offer. Four other England players on that tour were also tapped, and we were each asked to sign a form indicating our interests: no more, no less. It was not a binding contract, nor did it specifically mention sums of money or definite dates. So far as I know, all six of us signed.

My interest was genuine enough, but if a contract had

been offered I did not know what I would have done. I was well aware of the official attitude to team contact with South Africa. Obviously if such a scheme became public all hell would be let loose. Even in our tentative and hypothetical discussions, we were told to say nothing about the matter. We were also told to wait for further contact, and are still waiting. I can only assume that financial, organizational or political obstacles rendered the plan impossible –a fate which has happened so often to South African projects in the past decade.

I do not agree with apartheid: in fact, I am appalled by it. I accept that cricket in South Africa has probably broken down most of the barriers, within its own boundaries; but it can never be enough. My previous visit was in the winter of 1975–6. I played club cricket in Cape Town for a side called Greenpoint, who were the first in the area to include a coloured player. He was accepted into the bars, which was strictly illegal, and the police chose to ignore it. But outside the environs of the club, nothing changed: that same coloured cricketer could not have a drink with me in any city bar, and that, I thought, was pathetic. We were both humans, both entitled to the same sense of dignity, yet he was cast as a second-class citizen because the people who run South Africa are so insecure, so scared of losing what they have got.

I thought about these matters quite deeply during the West Indies trip, and after the approach. I could not decide how best to make a protest about South African policies. It is easy to say you will not go to the place, but it is a negative attitude, because nobody remembers you for it, or why you did it: public pronouncement from a distance are hollow. The best course, I felt, would be to go there – mix with, coach and play with the blacks and coloureds, and make my feelings known while in the country. Maybe I am naive to think it would have any effect, but at least it would be a positive gesture.

In general terms, I accept that the majority of cricketers would be attracted to South Africa for financial gain. I was no different, and fail to see what is wrong with the idea. Every week one can pick up a Sunday paper and read advertisements offering huge salaries for jobs in South African mines, or for administrative posts in their companies. There seems to be considerably less pressure on businessmen taking up these chances than on sportsmen taking up theirs. The difference is that sportsmen are in the public eye, an easy target for the demonstrators. But cricketers, just like businessmen, are free agents. If enough England players ever did want to go to South Africa as a team, protesters, let alone cricket officials, could do little to stop them earning their money.

Having heard no more about these plans, and not having been approached by John Edrich, I concentrated on trying to correct my Test form. Once again, I had been reprieved. There were a number of changes for the Old Trafford match, and again I would not have been surprised if I had been dropped. But on the first morning of Essex's weekend match, ironically against the Australians, Mike Brearley phoned to say I had been retained. I thought it significant that he told me I was 'in the twelve' rather than in the team. and was quite expecting to be left out on the morning of the match, although I later discovered that the twelfth-man position was always likely to rest between Gatting and Derek Underwood, one of three Kent players to be recalled.

Underwood was included because early reports from Manchester indicated that some turn was likely. Nobody, it seemed, had bothered to establish that it had poured with rain on an uncovered wicket and that it was bound to start damp! Chris Tavare came in at the expense of Peter Willey as the latest experiment in the number three slot, while Alan Knott returned to keep wicket. Bob Taylor was unlucky, and it could be said his omission was even unfair – he had done so little wrong – but nevertheless, I believe Knott, on form, is the best wicketkeeper–batsman I have ever seen. He was brought in for a specific purpose, to help win the Ashes, and the past and future were not considered relevant.

Coincidentally, news of the England squad was

welcomed enthusiastically in Essex, for the very good reason that we happened to have a Championship match against Kent at Chelmsford during the Test. The ball turned square and we won by an innings, but I wonder what might have happened had Underwood been among the opposition? The Essex revival had continued and we were still pursuing three honours, following a victory over Sussex in the NatWest Trophy quarter-final which might have astonished me but for my recent experiences at Leeds and Birmingham. It was a similar situation: we had not made enough runs and Sussex appeared to be cruising; then they lost their last five wickets for 21 runs. I felt I had read the script before.

I scored 86 against the Australians on Saturday and, despite being hit in the ribs quite painfully by Terry Alderman, went up to Manchester feeling a little more confident. My position, I knew, was not the only one at risk. David Gower was similarly short of runs, and so was Boycott, who began the game just a handful of runs away from becoming the highest-scoring England batsman of all time. Unusually, on the night before this game Boycott talked freely about the pressure all our batsmen were under each time they padded up. Once again we were discussing the sequence of first-innings flops which had made life so difficult for us in this series, and Geoff was clearly feeling as insecure as anyone.

The previous experiment with the order having failed, I was restored to open with Geoff, and felt more content there. But it made no difference, neither personally nor to the team. On a pitch which looked patchy but played well, we were bowled out for 230, and it might have been much worse but for a half-century from Lancashire's Paul Allott, making his Test début on his home ground. He played in the tail-end style of my Essex friend John Lever – up and down the line to anything straight, cutting loose when the bowler strayed. It was very effective and it avoided another complete disaster.

Following the established form of this series, Australia contrived to make our dismal efforts look formidable. Yet again, it was Bob Willis who caused their undoing with three wickets in an over at the start of the innings. The chanting which follows his pumping approach had by this stage become a ritual on all the Test grounds, and there is no doubt in my mind that it motivated Bob. He visibly responded to the involvement of the crowd; his moods, which can sometimes be crushingly low, were lifted to terrific peaks by the exhilaration of bowling in a way he thought he would never do again – and listening to the spectators revelling in it! The rest of us felt keyed up by him; the opposition, I can only assume, felt slightly unnerved by it all.

By Friday night, however, I had completed another miserable personal match, even though the game had three days left to run. I was out cheaply again, and by watching my dismissals on video replay, listening to the views of others and thinking deeply while batting, I believed I could finally put my finger on the reasons for my lack of form. Instead of not concentrating enough, as some people might have supposed, I was in fact concentrating too hard. Because of this I was moving before the bowler released the ball, and setting myself to play in a specific rigid way. Against Alderman, for example, I had taken to planting my front foot and playing around it. The bat was going back straight, but I was ending up playing across or around the line of flight. I knew I needed to relax and play more naturally, but with each Test innings I was finding that more difficult. I also knew, however, that the problem would now be taken out of my hands. Reprieves cannot go on for ever, and I was aware that I would be put out to grass in county cricket for what was left of the season.

We still had a game to win. I like to think I had retained the ability to put my problems aside in the dressing-room, because there is nothing more deflating for a team than listening to a depressed batsman moaning. I spent all the next day there, and from being one of the slowest days of Test cricket I had ever seen it suddenly changed gear in mid-afternoon because of another phenomenal performance from Botham.

Only 29 runs had been scored before lunch, of which Tavare had made nine. Chris seems to set himself to play that way in Test cricket, yet bats quite differently for Kent, striking the ball freely and improvising attractively. The pace did not change for the early part of the afternoon, and when Ian went in he spent twenty minutes gently adjusting, not aiming to hit anything with power; then he cut loose in quite amazing fashion. He had some luck early on, but very soon the Australians were finding it impossible to bowl to him. The longer he stayed, the worse they bowled, and it eventually became a complete massacre. It was as spectacular as Ian's 100 at Leeds, and technically better. In this innings he did not try to slog every ball out of the ground. He hit straighter and with more control, and it is the only way Ian should ever play; he is one of the very few cricketers in the world capable of such excesses, and I think that being an all-rounder helps him. A batsman, I believe, would never play in that fashion, simply because his innings is all he has got. If Ian fails, he does at least have his bowling to fall back on. But, having said that, the character of the man means that anything he does is performed in a spectacular way.

Botham gave the impetus, and Alan Knott maintained it with a typically impudent 50. He loves sweeping, and is equally adept at playing the shot square or fine. His judgement, indeed, was so good that Kim Hughes began to despair over where to put his fielders; each time he moved one to counter a Knott stroke, Alan would play the ball to a different part of the ground. The struggles of the early part of the day seemed remote, and by the close England were 430 ahead.

We added to it the next day, when John Emburey scored his first Test half-century. When I first knew John he was a genuine number eleven, but he has improved so much in recent years that he is now a good number eight or nine, perfectly capable of making regular twenties and thirties so long as he plays sensibly within his limitations. We were all out by lunchtime, and I was reminded of a comment Kim Hughes passed to Mike Brearley at Bob

Willis' benefit ball after the Edgbaston Test. 'We are no good at chasing 150,' he had said, 'but you set us 500, and we'll win.' He had the chance now.

Nothing looked less conceivable as Dyson was run out in the type of mid-wicket muddle which seems to follow Graeme Wood around, and then Wood himself was caught off Allott. Paul was having a memorable Test début, but his bowling ceased to look dangerous as the pitch and the batting improved on these last two days. Yallop won another battle with Willis and went on to play the best innings of the summer outside Botham's. He and Hughes played shots in a style which suggested they believed they could win: the runs came quickly, and the pitch now looked a beauty for batting. But three more wickets went down in the last session, and even at 210 for five Australia looked bound for defeat. Once more there had been a full house, an encouragement for the sponsors and administrators who wanted Sunday play. I know certain players object to having no rest day during a Test, but it is not something which bothers me, and I would certainly rather play before a big, enthusiastic Sunday crowd than the sparse gatherings Tests normally attract on Mondays.

It was symptomatic of a crazy series that the last day, the day on which England won the Ashes, starred an Australian. Their hero was Allan Border, consistently their best player, who made a fine century despite the obvious pain of a broken bone in his finger. He remained not out at the end, by which time Australia's apparently impossible mission had been reduced to an accessible level. Border was supported by Marsh and Lillee, the two old campaigners, and finally by Mike Whitney, the raw young bowler from Bondi who was dragged away from a county game at Cheltenham to play in his first Test, to nobody's greater surprise than his own.

In the end, of course, it was not enough. The catch which won the match, an extraordinary agile, reflex effort at slip to remove Lillee just as his stand with Border was beginning to threaten, was inevitably made by Roy of the

141

Rovers. It was impossible to keep Botham out of the game: he was man of the match for the third successive Test, and deserved it too. He was the player who had decided the Ashes, and in their long, competitive history I wonder if one cricketer has ever done quite so much towards the winning of a series.

14

Cushioning the Blow

The axe fell on Sunday, 23 August. England's team for the final Test at the Oval excluded both Gooch and Gower, the very pair who had returned from the West Indies just four months earlier lauded as the most exciting batsmen England had produced in a decade. Wayne Larkins of Northants and Paul Parker of Sussex were named as their replacements, and on the day the Test began Gooch and Gower were in ironical opposition at Colchester, where Essex were playing Leicestershire.

I heard the team announced on the radio. We were about to play a John Player League match against Northants at Milton Keynes, and I had been staying with Peter Willey, a closer friend since our weeks as room-mates in the Caribbean. When I returned to the team hotel there was a message in my pigeon-hole. Mike Brearley had phoned earlier that morning – a well-meaning call to cushion the blow, no doubt. I appreciated the thought, but in my case it was almost unnecessary. I had conditioned myself to expect to be left out, so I could not even say it was a disappointment. What I found much more surprising was David's omission. To my mind he had done no worse than almost everybody else in the preceding Tests, and he had played superbly in the West Indies. With a batsman of David's natural talent, I feel the selectors have to accept the inevitable, occasional bad patch, and persevere.

I suspect that neither of us in our hearts feared missing the Indian tour, nor do I supppose it was really in the minds of the selectors. But by playing Larkins and Parker they were giving themselves the opportunity to study two more players before sitting down to select the squad for the trip. I did not envy Wayne and Paul. Althought I am sure they were delighted to be picked, the pressure on them was enormous. It has happened many times before, and I am sure it will happen again, but the practice of introducing new players for the last Test of a home series, virtually putting them on trial, does seem unfair. If they fail, there is every chance they will miss out on the tour which follows, to the benefit of someone who was not considered good enough to play a week or so earlier. In many ways it is better for a fringe Test player to miss out at home; at least he then has no chance to fail before the tour squad is picked.

Even if the news had been a shock to me, it would have been difficult to be miserable for long – the Essex comedians would see to that. Milton Keynes' only previous experience of first-class cricket was the tour match against the West Indians in 1980, apparently played on a distinctly sporting track. Expecting something similar, John Lever and I solemnly marched to the middle carrying a stretcher we had found in the dressing-room. It amused the crowd, who were just settling in their seats, but I am not certain the groundsman saw the joke.

Every Sunday game was tense now; we won, to remain clear at the top of the league. The Championship match at Northampton was drawn, but I scored 146 and gleaned some lost confidence. Our chance of winning two honours, for the second time in three years, just about remained, but defeat at Derby the previous week had put paid to the dream of a treble. It was the NatWest Trophy semi-final, and we perpetuated our unwanted record of losing matches with the scores level. Twice before, in recent years, we had managed it, and this time it was a personal catastrophe for Nobby Phillip.

The match had dragged into a second damp day in the dingy surroundings of that most unloved county ground. We had been put in, and struggled for runs on a green pitch. It was Nobby who dragged us out of trouble, and

144

our final total of 149 represented a good recovery. By the end of the truncated first day we had removed Derbyshire's two star imports, Peter Kirsten and John Wright, and if anything the odds seemed to have swung our way. There was a shock for us the next morning: we arrived at the ground to discover that a lot of the grass had been taken off the pitch – much more than the regulation trim with a mower would have removed. It did not look the same, neither did it play the same. The ball had moved off the seam throughout the first day, but now there was only occasional deviation.

We did well to stay in the game, bowling and fielding superbly. A tumble of wickets brought us back from the dead, and the last pair were together when Nobby began the final over, six runs wanted. He dropped one short and it was hit for four, but with just one delivery left Derbyshire still needed a single to bring the scores level and win on the basis of fewer wickets lost. Nobby bowled the perfect delivery, right into the blockhole, and Paul Newman could only squeeze it straight back at him. The batsmen had to run, of course; but as Nobby picked up the ball and turned, Brian 'Lager' Hardie was positioned behind the stumps and Newman was yards out of his ground. It only needed a lob and we were in the final, but Nobby lost his head and hurled the ball at the stumps. He missed by some distance, and while Lager ripped off his sun hat and screwed it up in frustration, the Derbyshire crowd invaded, Newman performed a dance on the spot, and poor Nobby burst into tears. He had done something remarkably similar twice in an over during a John Player League match at Taunton three years earlier – but what a moment to stage an encore! Indomitably, we sang loudly in the dressing-room to drown the voice of Derbyshire captain Barry Wood as he was being interviewed in the corridor. But we all felt the defeat keenly. It had followed a disastrous four days in Hampshire, in which we had been beaten in the Championship and the John Player League, and suddenly our season, so rich in promise, was threatening poverty and ruin.

The Northampton game pulled us together, and the week at Colchester which followed calmed any nerves. We won both the Championship matches and the vital John Player fixture with Glamorgan, on the day that Keith Fletcher was confirmed as England captain for the Indian tour. It had been heavily rumoured for weeks before, and I knew how badly Fletch wanted the job – especially in India, which he loves. Alec Bedser phoned him on the Saturday morning, and he told most of us quietly during the day. He warned that there would inevitably be a lot of press and television fuss when the announcement was made, but that he meant to keep us all out of the way. There would be enough pressure on us with Sunday's game to be won. In the event, Fletch handled his personal pressures, and the team's, as capably as ever, although there was one typical Essex moment of humour as he led us out to field. Peter Edwards, our secretary, was announcing the England appointment over the public address system, and as the crowd stood to cheer Fletch self-consciously dropped his head and kept walking. What he did not know was that we had all stopped on the boundary edge and were convulsed with giggles as he marched to the middle quite alone.

That week at Colchester restored my form – not that it had ever been bad at county level. My scores were 75, 105, 16, 42 and 117. Within the space of a week I had scored three Championship centuries and corrected most of the minor technical faults which had been afflicting my game. Correcting them, in fact, was straightforward; the hard part had been pinpointing where the fault lay. Now I was standing straighter, and waiting for the ball instead of committing myself to a forward move. I felt less tense, the freedom and spontaneity returned, and I began to enjoy batting again. It was a good feeling.

There was, of course, a psychological hurdle to clear. It was impossible to forget that England were playing elsewhere, without me, and I was fascinated by my own reaction to it. It was the first time I had been left out by England since December 1979, and eighteen consecutive

Tests accustom you to a routine. Someone reminded me on the Wednesday afternoon that the boys would be at nets, and for a moment it did feel strange to be absent. It was interesting to watch some of the Test on television as a detached spectator, and I inevitably had mixed feelings on the Thursday morning. The reassuring suspicion that I would be back for the tour was a help. Had I imagined that I faced a lengthy spell away from the Test scene, I would undoubtedly have felt more sharply that I was missing it.

The Colchester Festival ended with a magnificent last day against Glamorgan. We thought we had set them an impossible target – more than 400 – on one of the cruellest turning pitches I have seen. But Javed Miandad batted as if he was facing underarms with a tennis ball on the beach. If anyone in the Essex side doubted that he is one of the world's greats, he proved it that day with 200 not out. It was one of the finest innings I have ever seen, and it gave us an almighty scare before John Lever returned to take two wickets in the closing overs and we sneaked in by a handful of runs. Javed was dropped four times, including once by me at slip. It split my finger and I had it stitched in the dressing-room by a hastily summoned doctor – our physio had gone to hospital with our first invalid, Brian Hardie, who had taken a blow in the jaw at short leg.

Despite this string of good results Essex were making no impression on the Championship leaders, Notts, who kept winning game after game with remorseless efficiency. The cry was going up all round England that their policy of making flagrantly green wickets at Trent Bridge was unethical, but far more remarkable was the fact that Clive Rice seemed to win the toss for every home game, and inevitably bowl first.

The Test season was over. Our title bid looked to have faded. There was still the matter of the John Player League to settle, though, and we knew that if we won our two remaining games we would be the champions for the first time. We headed for Scarborough, and the perennially good atmosphere of the Festival. Unfashionable it may be, and in some cases an unwanted extra fixture for the players, but Scarborough has a special appeal matched by no other cricket centre. The hotels are always full of people, most of whom are there purely for the Festival, and the faces seem to be the same year after year. The ground is my favourite in Yorkshire; big crowds, short boundaries and a pitch which always plays well despite being green. A band plays during the tea interval, and the players can look forward to fish and chips on the promenade each evening.

The Fenner Trophy, the limited-over knockout competition which annually involves four counties, has sometimes been devalued in the past by teams agreeing to split the prize money and consequently not being too anxious about the outcome. But Fletch told us when we arrived that we were not playing to those rules. We wanted to win, he said, and we would play properly and take whatever money was due to us at the end of the week. It was an attitude with which I agreed completely, because festivals and competitions of this nature will not survive unless they are played competitively. We won our semi-final on Wednesday and spent the next day playing golf on the championship course at Ganton. Nine of us played, and we managed to lose thirty-two balls between us, of which my substantial share was eight. The final, on the Friday, was an exciting, high-scoring contest which we lost by just two runs to Yorkshire. It pleased the locals, but it did not please our captain, who has never been very much in love with that part of the world.

By the time we set off for home, and the four-and-a-half-hour drive which emphasizes the logistic drawback to Scarborough, most of us were thinking ahead to the match with Middlesex on Sunday. So often in the past Essex had missed out in the John Player League through a single defeat at a crucial time. Three times we had been runners-up, on two occasions when our points were equal to those of the winners, so this time the entire club was determined to let nothing slip. Chelmsford was packed and Middlesex were no obliging pushovers. With three

148

overs left we still wanted 18 to win, and I was reminded of a similar situation four years earlier, when again we had needed to win our last two games but had lost to Yorkshire – at Scarborough. This time, Kenny McEwan saw us through, taking 12 runs off the thirty-eighth over and easing the pressure. He went on to a century, but with three still required from the final over the tension in our dressing-room was indescribable. Derek Pringle had to go in with three balls left and a single needed, and to a great roar of relief from the crowd and ourselves he squirted his first ball down to third man to put us out of our misery.

The following morning Alec Bedser discharged his last job as chairman of selectors by naming the squad to tour India and Sri Lanka. It is nice to see your name on the list, even if it is no surprise, and I was equally pleased that John Lever was back. He has the capacity for a lot of hard work, and no doubt he was picked partly for his record in India, where the ball moves more in the air than off the pitch. But more important than that, to my mind, are his other qualities on tour. He has a natural ability to be funny and cheerful almost all the time, an ideal person to have around when things get rough. Geoff Cook's inclusion was probably the nearest thing to a surprise, and in view of the political wrangling which followed it was a controversial choice in more ways than one. Purely on the playing front, he had ironically benefited from his Northants team-mate Wayne Larkins' relative failure in the Oval Test. Graham Dilley was brought back, which raised a few eyebrows as he had so lost form and confidence that he could hardly take a wicket in Kent's second team towards the end of the summer. But he remains the only young, genuinely fast bowler England possess. He has ability, and only his temperament is suspect; if the captain can bring out his true potential he must always play. If only Graham had more self-confidence there are few limits to what he could achieve. Most of the current England bowlers are the same men who were doing service five years ago, and they are all now over thirty; there is a desperate shortage of good quick bowlers of around twenty-five.

The position of second wicketkeeper is always cause of much debate, and I feel it is often a wasted place on tour. Jack Richards of Surrey got the job this time, and he was probably lucky that the decision to take seven batsmen, instead of the customary six, meant that the selectors could choose him on keeping ability alone. Alan Knott was again unavailable, which was a pity, but I did not agree that he should not be considered at Test level again. In my opinion he remains the best we have, and unless someone of similar standing emerges, who is willing to tour each year, I see nothing against recalling Knotty for home series. Players should not be penalized for making the decision not to tour – the strain of leaving home and family for three or four months every winter is considerable.

I had two more Championship matches to play for Essex, and in the first of them, at Taunton, I found myself leading the side for the first time in a first-class game. Fletch was resting an injury and Ray East, the vice-captain, was not selected, so I went out to toss, won, and put Somerset in. I thought it the right decision because the pitch was like most people's front lawn and virtually indistinguishable from the rest of the square, but it turned out to be an inauspicious start to my captaincy career for Somerset scored more than 400 on the first day. Viv Richards scored a century, playing masterfully after some early good luck, and Ian Botham then smashed the ball around the ground in a style all too familiar to me – usually I have been on the right side, though! I began to realize the agonies Kim Hughes must have gone through at Headingley and Old Trafford, because I simply ran out of ideas about how to stop Ian. I put on David Acfield – who reported laconically later, 'It was either him or me, and he was captain' – and pushed nine men on to the fence. Eventually, Ian did hole out – but the cost was high. Several hours were lost to rain, but we still had a fight to save the game on the final day, and I was pleased to achieve something positive with a century – a painful one, however, as I finished with bruises on my shoulder, ribs and head.

The season ended at the Oval. It is not, in the normal course of events, an atmospheric ground, but on the Sunday which decided the John Player League it was alive with tension and resounded to the chants and songs of Essex supporters. It was as good as a home game for us: there were 10,000 people in and I reckon all but a few hundred were from Essex. Throughout the season we had enjoyed large and regular support, and when the crunch came the fans excelled themselves. We knew that, if we won, we were champions. If we lost, we had to rely on Warwickshire losing at Taunton. The tannoy kept us up to date with the other match throughout the afternoon, and it was quickly evident that Somerset were doing us a favour. But we still wanted to end in style – and we did.

Nothing was more apt than the playing of the hero's role by Nobby Phillip, villain of the NatWest disaster. He went in to bat when we were a little behind the scoring rate we would have liked, and proceeded to assault each bowler with great relish. He ensured a challenging score; it only became a formidable one after a very strange interruption. Play had begun a few minutes late due to rain, and the game had been reduced to 39 overs per side. But at ten minutes past four Surrey were still bowling the thirty-eighth over and Stuart Turner, who was batting with Nobby, asked one of the umpires whether this would be the last over. He was told it would, so attempted an impossible extra run off the last ball and was run out. All the players trooped off, the television cameras switched to another event, and the scoreboard operators began turning the board back to blank. But upstairs in the umpires' room Keith Fletcher was pointing out that they were wrong and that, if a match is reduced in length, the revised amount of overs must be bowled regardless of the time. He was right, the umpires conceded, and so after the weirdest of five-minute breaks the same players went back on the field – minus poor Stuart – and Nobby proceeded to take

19 runs off the extra over. It was a Botham-type innings, an enormous relief to Nobby, the nervous Dominican, and a hammer-blow to Surrey. They were set more than 200 and never looked likely to get them. Before seven o'clock, we were drinking champagne on the Oval balcony.

15

Another Sad Farewell

Rumours that England's winter tour of India and Sri Lanka would be cancelled had first been prompted by the Jackman crisis in Guyana, way back in February. They had been refuelled at various stages of the summer by some statements from obscure Indian sources deploring the links of certain English cricketers with South Africa. No one, it seemed, was willing to say anything official, and the Test and County Cricket Board adopted a stoical British stance and assumed all was well unless they heard otherwise. They heard on Friday, 16 October. More than five weeks after the announcement of the tour squad, and its acceptance by the Indian Cricket Board, official government sources in India were reported as stating that their country could not allow Geoff Boycott or Geoff Cook to play in the party. Boycott had paid vacational visits to South Africa and coached there, and Cook had spent the previous winter captaining Eastern Province in the Currie Cup. A fortnight of frantic speculation followed, in which for long periods the tour appeared inevitably doomed. But on 29 October, clearly after directions from Prime Minister Mrs Indira Gandhi herself, the Indians gave the tour an unconditional all-clear – Boycott, Cook and all.

Back at Chadwell Heath, in training again with West Ham, nothing seemed to have changed. In fact one thing had changed, as the boys were this season battling it out with the big guns of Division One rather than running away with the Second Division; but for me the pattern of emotions was very similar to that of ten months earlier. I was due for more than three months overseas, and I was not entirely sure I liked the idea. So when the threat of the tour we had all half expected became reality, my feelings were confusingly mixed. If the threat was carried through and the tour abandoned, I was well aware of the consequences for world cricket: utter turmoil; two camps – black playing black, white playing white, and ne'er the twain shall meet. It was too close for comfort now, and once that split occurred, it would take an awful lot of patching together. But selfishly, blocking from my mind the international considerations, the thought of a winter at home was not at all unappealing. So I waited, knowing nothing more than the man in the street. When one or other of the West Ham players asked me whether we were going, I had to say I didn't know. There had been no word from the TCCB, because there was little they could tell us. Privately, however, I felt 90 per cent sure it would be off – the Indian protests seemed too official and too strong for any other outcome.

Quite apart from the undeniable fact that the Indians had left their objection extremely late – news reached the English authorities only nineteen days before we were due to fly out – the whole thing smacked of double standards. Most members of the Indian team who were to provide our opposition had not only played with or against Boycott and Cook in England, but had also played with or against South Africans. Take Kapil Dev, currently the star of the Indian side, their equivalent of our Botham: he is now a Northants player, so is captained by Cook, and he goes on to the field with Allan Lamb, who was born and brought up in South Africa despite his residential qualification for England. Perhaps the greatest hypocrisy of all concerned Tony Greig, captain of the last England team to tour India, in 1976–7. The crowds adored him wherever he went, and he apparently did much to ensure that the series was conducted in the best possible spirit. But Greig, too, had been born in South Africa. So what had changed since? And why?

Then I heard on the radio that the tour was on after all. Whether or not the two governments had consulted I will never know – nor did I particularly care. What concerned me was that the news came through on Friday afternoon, giving me precisely five days before the squad meeting at Lord's the following Wednesday – five days in which to squeeze all the preparations I would normally have made over a period of about five weeks. Perhaps more important, I had to come to terms with the tour ahead. It had been easy in the preceding weeks to become resigned to staying in England. The sudden realization that after all the uncertainty I had to pack up and fly off again, to spend another three and a half months in unfamiliar parts, was not easy to cope with.

In one sense I was pleased to be going, because playing cricket for England is my livelihood and my main job incentive: I get a kick out of playing for my country. I really do feel proud to be opening the innings against the best bowlers from around the world, and there are few better feelings than scoring a century in a Test. Also, without wishing people to accuse me of being cynical, the financial rewards are far greater than I could hope to command if I left Test cricket. But I still believe some qualms about touring must lurk in the mind of every cricketer, however gregarious and ambitious he is. Very few men, certainly if they are married, can relish such a long period away from home, especially when the prospect is an annual repeat for as long as they are good enough to keep a Test place. Some players love touring; they thrive on the hotel life and the strange places. Others dislike it, suffer from homesickness and boredom, but keep going because they know it is the best job they are likely to hold down. I would not categorize myself in either of these extremes, but I could never envisage touring for as many years as some of the current England team. Before the tour of India Bob Willis was about to embark on his eighth winter away in the last nine, and for Derek Underwood it was to be his ninth in the last eleven. I admire them for it, but do not wish to emulate them.

Perhaps my doubts this time were caused as much by a mistrust of India itself as by anything else. I had been there only briefly, for the Jubilee Test at Bombay in 1980, but I knew enough to feel that the country did not suit me. I knew that the game was very different from anything English players are used to, and that visiting cricketers are treated like idols by the Indian public. But I also knew that the organization could sometimes irritate, and that Indian umpires could outrage players. Given the choice, I would always opt for Western comfort and English food, and the prospect of three months away from both was daunting. My appetite for Indian food had never stretched beyond the occasional attempt at a tandoori chicken, and for all the reassurances I heard about the standards of modern hotels in Indian cities, I approached departure day with deep apprehension. It was odd that I should worry, because my two Essex team-mates in the party, Keith Fletcher and John Lever, are both great fans of India. Fletch was making his third full tour there and rates it the best place in the world to play cricket, and John – who played under Greig five years ago – told me he enjoyed it immensely. I remained unconvinced.

My hectic schedule in those final few days at home might have been sheer bedlam but for the fact that I had already turned down a number of invitations to attend or speak at local functions. I may have upset one or two people, but it was a decision based on past experience. There is little enough time between the end of an English season and the start of a tour, and if I took up all the offers and invitations put my way I would be out four or five nights a week immediately before going away, which is not fair on Brenda.

My packing was not helped by the fact that my official tour kit had not arrived; when it did appear, the blazer did not fit. I tried to cut down on my luggage, because in the past I have generally taken too many clothes, but there were still various important extras to squeeze in. I also took some currant cakes – a particular favourite of mine which I did not think would be freely available in places like Nagpur and Baroda – and six bottles of red wine, because during the Jubilee Test visit I had decided to sample the local wine one evening and found myself charged £10 per bottle for pure firewater.

We had been told to gather at Lord's earlier than usual, and I had my suspicions about the reason. They were amply confirmed by the sight of television cameras, and although Raman Subba Row, the manager, was straight-faced and serious as he told us they were making a documentary film, it was not long before Eamonn Andrews appeared with a big red book: Ian Botham – who had fortunately not suspected anything – was to be the subject of that week's *This Is Your Life*. Graham Dilley gave an amusing and very passable impression of Eamonn which even went down with the man himself, and the programme was recorded slickly. Then, after the official business was conducted, we left for the Aldwych, and a reception at the Indian High Commission, followed by the usual farewell dinner at Lord's.

We spent the night at the Excelsior Hotel at Heathrow before boarding the morning flight for Bombay. From Heathrow to Bombay takes just over eight hours, non-stop, and is a good deal more merciful than the draining flight to Australia, even if my personal preference is for the tours down under. Boredom is the greatest enemy in the air, and I noticed that almost half the squad had this year brought modern, Walkman stereos with headphones, and sat in a world of their own, only the drumming fingers or tapping feet giving a slight clue to their musical prefer-ences. It was an uneventful journey but for one minor flap just as the plane began to dip into Bombay. Bob Willis suddenly discovered that his wallet was missing, contain-ing most of his important documents quite apart from his money. For a few minutes the entire squad was turned into a search party, until a somewhat shame-faced Goose announced that he had found the missing item in his own holdall!

For anyone new to India – and there were several among our number – the welcome we received at the airport must have seemed staggering. For those of us who had been before, it would perhaps have been a surprise if it had been absent. There were garlands and flowers for us all, and hundreds of well-wishers pointing and staring as if we were beings from another planet – and this despite the fact that it was two o'clock in the morning. We came to expect such receptions at every stop around this extraordinarily cricket-crazy country.

Our first home was the Taj Mahal Hotel, which looks out on the sea, and the monument known as the Gateway of India, and is without doubt as good as any hotel in the world. A new wing had been added recently, but we were all given rooms in the old, traditional part, where everything is high-ceilinged and elegant. If the décor was typically Indian, the facilities could let you imagine yourself anywhere in the world. I had decided to avoid Indian food, partly because I did not like the little I knew of it and partly, I admit, because I was suspicious of the stomach troubles it might cause those unused to it. I contented myself with the excellent varieties of Chinese food available at the Taj and, more surprisingly, at most hotels we visited.

My own foibles and fancies were mild compared to some. I shared a room with Chris Tavare of Kent, who was making his first England tour. Tav is by nature quiet and reserved, even a little studious – as befits one who has an Oxford University degree in zoology . We soon found that he did not like sitting in the sun and was very choosy about his food. When I noticed that he also took a variety of pills to prevent most known diseases, it was quite obvious that he had been thoroughly briefed by his county team-mate Alan Knott, notorious as the most fanatically careful and vigilant of all cricketers when it comes to diet, health and fitness.

Of the other newcomers, Geoff Cook with his easy manner and dry humour proved the good tourist we all assumed he would be, wicketkeeper Jack Richards was chatty, bright and bouncy, and Lancashire's Paul Allott was splendid company. The party began to gel encouragingly, with Fletch making it plain that he wanted people to enjoy themselves, but would tread firmly on anyone who stepped out of line. He was immensely popular with the lads from the start, as was our most diplomatic manager. In the sad absence of Ken Barrington, the duties of organizing net sessions were taken on by Bob Willis, and were handled expertly in the sticky 90-degree heat of Bombay.

John Emburey experienced the frustrations of India in one of those episodes which seem so maddening to the victim, yet so hilarious to everyone else. John's wife Suzy was spending the first part of the winter in her native Australia, and all his efforts to phone her via the hotel switchboard were beset with problems. They simply could not get through to the number. Resigning himself to the fact that Indian communications were to blame, John forgot about it until he picked up his bill at the end of the stay. A charge had been made for the call they were unable to connect, and printed alongside was the number – not in Australia, but in Austria!

Once we left Bombay and set off around the country, we quickly came to know the family of Indians responsible for our baggage. The job of transporting our mountain of trunks between bases was done by a man named Govind and his two sons, and it was their proud boast that they had never lost a bag in all the years they had been working with teams visiting their country. They travelled everywhere by train, so there was sometimes a considerable wait for fresh clothes after we had arrived by plane, but they were marvellously reliable – and humble. They slept each night on mattresses outside the manager's room and clearly thought this was their place. In Nagpur, Raman found that he had a spare bed in his room and offered it to Govind, but the old man politely refused and settled for another night on the floor.

One of the most alarming features of India is the driving, particularly by the taxi-drivers. Perhaps it is the urgency to complete one fare and get on to the next (the queue of taxis at Bombay airport stretches back miles and the drivers there are lucky if they pick up one fare a day), but they all appear to drive like madmen. Hand on horn, they plunge in and out of the traffic as if it was a fairground dodgem circuit. Accidents seem to be miraculously avoided by a hair's breadth at each corner, making no difference whatever to the mood or the speed of the driver, and the best way to survive the experience without bringing on heart trouble is by shutting your eyes. The golden rule, certainly, is never to sit in the front!

It is always a relief to get into the cricket after all the preliminaries, and our first match was a one-day game at the old Test ground in Bombay, the Brabourne Stadium. Despite its dilapidated appearance on the outside, the ground was in good shape, and 35,000 people packed in to watch us win. We enjoyed that more than the dinner which followed. Seven people stood up to speak, most of them at considerable length.

The journey to Pune, for our first three-day game, was completed by train and was an education in itself. The train took about seven hours, but stopped only three times, and at each station around four hundred people were crowded on to the platform to catch a glimpse of us. Living in England, with its ready transport links to all parts and its frequent international sporting events, it is hard to appreciate that these people in the villages of India had probably never set eyes on a Test cricketer before, and that to them this was something very special. Our carriage was first-class, which meant it was tolerably comfortable. It was diverting to look out of the window at the commuter trains, which were so packed that dozens of people were literally hanging out of each carriage.

We won the match in Pune on a belter of a batting wicket, and and it was frustrating for me to miss the game. Instead, I watched the England badminton team, who by some remarkable coincidence happened to be playing just down the road. Ray Stevens, our number one male player, lives in Ilford and we had met before. I also played a little golf in Pune, though this too was a frustration. My caddy's name was Iqbal, and on one particular hole he managed to direct me on to the wrong green. Needless to say, I lost.

Most of us had by now experienced mild stomach trouble, but illness struck seriously for the first time in Pune, and the victim was poor Bob Willis, so often an early casualty when there are any viruses to be had. He shook it off within a few days, which was just as well because our next stop was Nagpur, hardly a convivial spot in which to feel rough. Our accommodation there was described, quaintly, as a government circuit house, but in fact consisted of a compound of huts which appeared to be open house for the odd rat from the neighbourhood. We slept on rock-hard beds under mosquito nets, and the primitive conditions did not endear themselves to my two roommates, Tav and Geoff Boycott. The food, too, was appalling. Those, who had been there five years earlier were surprised, as they recalled feeding very well on Chinese food in the marquee erected for us. This time the marquee was the same, but the cook had been changed – for the worse. Most of the lads lived off eggs, and my diet consisted mainly of oranges and the tinned meat we had shipped out with us.

Another round of golf had its eccentric moments. We played on browns – rolled mud – next to a school, and had not got very far round when some five hundred youngsters converged on us, along with their teacher. There was no way that we could continue amid the clamour, and our mild protests to the teacher only brought the bland response: 'We are all bunking, sir. . . .'

The wicket at Nagpur was a minefield for batting, and I did not get going in either innings, but we managed to win again and left the place able to laugh at the hazards and mishaps. We arrived at Baroda, where the Express Hotel seemed like heaven after the circuit house. This was our last first-class game before the First Test in Bombay, and an important one for me. I badly wanted a long innings, but it was not to be. In the Maharajah's grounds, a short throw from the crocodile lake, I was twice given out l.b.w., having hit them both quite hard. It will inevitably seem like sour grapes, but I cannot believe that the umpiring standards in India are good. Their decisions are inconsistent, sometimes apparently based on excitable temperaments, although I would never suggest they were biased. It was a problem we were to be affected by increasingly in the weeks to follow.

We travelled by coach to Ahmedabad, scene of a one-day international just two days before the Test, and on the road Paul Allott's cask of white wine was passed around to while away the time in a pleasant manner. This time the hotel and ground were both good, and although the crowd was fiercely partisan, almost intimidatingly so, we came through it well and won the match by five wickets. It had not always looked to be that comfortable. Chasing only 156, we had slumped from 40 for one to 60 for four, but Fletch and Mike Gatting did the donkey work and Roy of the Rovers arrived in typical style, for the finale. With 12 wanted to win in three overs, Ian Botham launched into the attack, was dropped at long-on and then hit the next two deliveries for six. It was the sort of thing that is difficult to watch if you are next in, but undeniably effective. The man of the match award deservedly went to Gatt for his cool and composed 47 not out. But, with a baffling logic, the adjudicators then made India's Dilip Vengsarkar batsman of the match for his 48.

My form was clearly causing some concern, not least to myself. Just as I was a few months earlier, I felt confident enough, yet consistently failed to build an innings. I had not been out in single figures on the trip, but neither had I passed 25, and it was obviously worrying. Early on I had been out to some poor shots; the umpiring decisions in Baroda had not helped; and at Ahmedabad, where I had felt unusually nervous, I had been caught down the leg-side. Quite how much one had to do with the other I don't know, but apart from suffering poor form I was also a little depressed because India had not, so far at least, agreed with me. I was in the Test side, however, and grateful for it, though it seemed ironically inevitable when I began to feel ill on the afternoon before the game began. I spent a few hours in bed, missing out on the governor's tea party, but roused myself in time for the team dinner, where I saw

Graham Dilley and Bob Willis both make early exits from the table suffering from something similar.

This was a Test we could not afford to lose; a Test, too, in which my own reputation was at stake again. I just hoped that my luck and my form would turn. But it was a vain hope. . . .

16

The Curtain Falls

Cricket can destroy its heroes as dramatically as they are created, and Graham Gooch entered the Test series in India late in November with his international future at stake. For him, as for England, things were to get worse before they got better. The Bombay Test was lost humiliatingly, amid acrimonious feelings over the Indian umpires. Gooch, desperate for runs, failed twice in the match and his depression intensified. But gradually the talent of the man, which none disputed, found its way to the surface. The 1981 year was not to end under such a dark cloud after all.

How does a defeated team protest about incompetent umpiring without inviting accusations of sour grapes? This was the dilemna faced by our tour management in Bombay. Even before the Test began Raman Subba Row had lodged a complaint with the Indian Board of Control, directed at the general standard of umpiring in our matches so far, but in the Test itself we felt a new low was achieved. The number of debatable decisions grew virtually with each session of play, and our confidence was inevitably damaged, hard as we tried to convince ourselves that we should put all thoughts of the umpires out of our heads. It must however be admitted that England did not deserve anything but defeat. Our batsmen, myself included, gave what will justifiably be considered one of the worst performances seen by an England side in recent years, and as the mandatory firecrackers and fruit missiles exploded all around us to celebrate India's triumph on the fourth afternoon, we were left to reflect that this was the fifth consecutive Test series we had begun with a defeat.

Such gloomy thoughts had seemed a remote prospect on the first evening of the match. We had lost the toss, yet produced a very good effort in the field to dismiss India for only 179. Although the wicket was confirming its uneven appearance and offering every bowler some assistance, this was a better start then we could even have hoped for; it was due in no small way to a colossal effort from Ian Botham, who bowled unchanged for four and a half hours and picked up four wickets. Unhappily, I was to end the day feeling still less secure than before. Given an uncomfortable half-hour to bat, I survived less than two overs before being bowled by Madan Lal for two. My only comfort was that, even as my personal tour threatened to develop into a nightmare of the blackest type, the team was shaping well. This, I felt instinctively, was a series we ought to win.

All that changed within twenty-four hours. Day two began contentedly enough, as Boycott and Tavare inched their uncompromising path to 95 for one, with the usual simmering full-house crowd of 50,000 showing more patience than I would have imagined possible. But as soon as Boycott departed the collapse was underway. David Gower was run out, and there followed a horrifying period in which three of our middle-order men, playing the sweep shot, were adjudged l.b.w. These were decisions which would have raised eyebrows anywhere, particularly as the ball was turning, but to us they seemed especially distressing in view of the repeated rejections our own appeals had suffered the previous day.

We were all out for 166, and Keith Fletcher called a team meeting that evening. His comments were forthright and necessary: he told us that the match was still there to be won, but that we must forget about the umpiring before our fears developed into a complex; he also stressed that we needed to keep India's second-innings lead down to about the 200 mark if we were to stay in the game. It looked for some time as if we would succeed. By lunch on the third day India had lost five wickets and were little more than 100 ahead. But the lower order proved more resistant, and by the close their lead had been extended to 216 with the last pair together. It was perfectly poised.

India is not the type of country in which anything riotous can occur during evenings or rest days, since there is very little to do. Our regular routine consisted of a drink in the team room or the hotel bar, a meal, reading a book and falling asleep. But on the night of the rest day we were at least able to vary the schedule as the hotel staff and BBC technicians succeeded in inducing some life from the video machine we had brought out with us. We treated ourselves to the recorded highlights of England's soccer victory over Hungary – good, patriotic stuff, just right for the rigours ahead.

It made no difference, however. India's last pair added another 24 runs and we were set to score 240: difficult, certainly, but not impossible, we thought – but within a couple of hours it was all over. Madan Lal, a big-hearted medium-pacer but not the sort of bowler who should ever run through a Test-class batting side, had taken five for 20 and we had been hustled out in an embarrassing fashion. The collapse had begun with my dismissal to the fourth ball of the innings, and I now knew that I was again under severe pressure for my place. My confidence was once more as low as it had been during the darkest days of the summer. What a year of contrasts this was turning out to be!

We travelled south to Hyderabad in low spirits. The lads knew just how hard it would be to win the series from one down. The Indians, who seldom play cricket in a belligerent manner anyway, would now give nothing away – although, at the time, we could not have imagined quite to what extent they would go to slow down proceedings in the forthcoming Tests.

My own wheel of fortune began to spin in the game against South Zone. I made an unbeaten century on the second day, and the feel of the ball striking the middle of the bat was reassuring after such a run of low scores. I felt particularly sorry for Geoff Cook: his chances were necessarily limited on this trip, and he was out first ball when he came in at number three for his only innings of the game. Fletch was at the centre of things for much of this match,. He declared behind and then bowled a long spell of leg-breaks to encourage a response from South Zone. Their declaration left us with little chance of winning the game, but a good and valuable opportunity for batting practice. Fletch opened himself and scored 100, and with half an hour left wandered down the pitch to tell John Emburey, his partner, that he intended to make use of the time by practising the sweep shot. He connected with a few, and in another mid-wicket conference passed the comment to Emburey that the umpire struck him as one of the best we had seen. It was asking for trouble, of course, and two calls later, sweeping again, Fletch was given out l.b.w.

The flight to Bangalore, venue for the next Test, was preceded by an egg-and-chip supper in the dressing-room. Neither Ian Botham nor Bob Willis was able to enjoy it, as both were suffering from stomach trouble; poor Bob had not managed to shake it off since the early weeks of the trip, and now looked like missing the Second Test. One long-standing tradition was abandoned in Bangalore: the captain decided that the team dinner on the eve of Tests was pointless on tour, as the players were together all the time anyway and would probably prefer to choose their own menu and eat at their leisure. We did, of course, hold a pre-match meeting at which our team and tactics were discussed. John Emburey had been left out so that we could play an extra batsman – a regrettable but essential measure after the events of Bombay – and there was some talk of changing the order if I was first out, to prevent Fiery and Chris Tavare batting together in their similarly defensive styles. This was thrown out, rightly I feel, because no batsman likes to sit in the dressing-room not knowing whether he is in next or not. Boycott and Tavare are good for the balance of the side, set against the more positive approach of players such as David Gower, Ian Botham and myself, and if they occasionally obstructed quick progress by their methods it was a cross we had to bear.

167

Willis failed to convince anyone that he was fit enough to play, so John Lever was brought in. His first contribution was as nightwatchman, twenty minutes from the end of a typical day of Test cricket in India: runs came slowly, and overs were bowled at snail's pace. Boycott and I had put on 90 for the first wicket, my return to some sort of form continuing, but from that promising platform we failed to consolidate, and the close score of 181 for four was a disappointment. Tavare had taken an age to score 22, batting one entire session for the addition of only nine, and much as I respected and appreciated the way in which he had dedicated himself to building Test innings and, ultimately, a long international career, I felt this might be taking things a little far. I have mentioned that by nature he is retiring, and our nickname experts had by now christened him Rowdy – a direct pinch from the Australians' nickname for their similarly silent Ashley Mallett.

We managed some acceleration the next day and the innings ended right on stumps with the total on 400. Gower, Botham and Dilley had all made half-centuries, but the day was not without its anger and controversy, provided surprisingly by our captain. Keith's frustration had clearly been building over the amount of apparently dubious decisions he had been given on the trip, and he momentarily boiled over when he was adjudged caught behind down the leg-side from a ball which he thought had clipped only his pad. As he started off back to the pavilion, he flicked one stump with his bat, knocking off the bails. It was a bad-tempered act seen plainly by everyone on the ground; it was also very out of character, but symptomatic of the pressures we were playing under. Fletch apologized the following morning at his rest-day press conference.

Ian Botham was named BBC Sports Personality of the Year on the second evening of the game, and a direct link to London was set up by the television crew. It was an entertaining session, and champagne was provided to toast a man who had suffered his own share of lows this

year before touching the peaks. Ian did us all a favour
when he announced on television that we were missing
decent English beer; the next day a telegram arrived from
Webster's brewery, informing us that forty dozen cases of
Yorkshire bitter were on the way.

To have any prospect of winning the game we had to
bowl out India for 200 or less and impose the follow-on,
but it never looked remotely likely. They made 189 for one
on the third day, when Sunil Gavaskar battled through
the day for 71, and by the end of the fourth day it was
England who faced the only possibility of defeat. Gavaskar had marched grimly on to 163 not out, and India
were five runs ahead with three wickets left. Another
50-odd added on the final morning, and we would be
under some pressure. But thankfully the worst did not
happen: we took the last three wickets quite cheaply, and
the final day contained not a hint of drama as we comfortably batted out time. It was, in conclusion, a Test which had
seemed destined for stalemate. The pitch was true and flat,
India were content with the draw, and without Willis we did
not have the scope to aim for anything ambitious.

After the dry, burning heat of the south, we now set off
on a long, arduous journey north into the foothills of the
Himalayas, to Jammu. We flew first to Delhi, where
Fletcher, Taylor and Underwood stayed behind while the
rest of us suffered a 4 a.m. call for the one daily flight to the
venue for our game against North Zone. We had been
warned that the cold might surprise us, and indeed we
needed two sweaters on all day. I shared a room with John
Emburey, and we kept our electric fire on throughout our
stay. We scarcely left the hotel other than to go to the
ground, and our evening entertainment consisted of a
form of charades which was often very amusing, particularly the manager's improbable mime of the television
detective Kojak. Brenda's birthday fell during our stay
there and I decided to attempt a phone call home, without
much hope of success. It took me twenty minutes to
explain to the operator which number I wanted in England, and that I wanted the call between midday and

2 p.m., Indian time, so as to catch Brenda before she left for work. But only five minutes after I had replaced the receiver it rang, and the gentleman proudly told me that I was through. It was only four in the morning in England and I don't think Brenda was very impressed, but it was still better than not talking to her at all.

The match was played on a dry, powdery pitch which always looked likely to help the bowlers, and we dismissed North Zone for 167, replying with 73 without loss on the first evening. Both Geoff Boycott and I were reprieved by the umpires after what seemed very good leg-before appeals, and I wandered down the pitch to mutter: 'We're two in credit there, Fiery.' 'Aye,' he said, 'but they still owe me two more yet!'

Following the last day of the game, which faded quietly into a draw, the hotel laid on a special party for us. The one problem was that they advertised it as a partners' evening, and of course none of us was at the time accompanied by wives or girlfriends. Ian Botham, however, announced that he had a partner for the event, and made a grand entrance into the team-room early that evening with a lady on his arm . . . or was it a lady? No, it was John Lever dressed in full drag! They carried the performance through, sweeping into the function together, and gathering looks of total bewilderment from the locals.

Our next engagement was a one-day international in Jullundur, centre of India's sports goods industry. I had been given the name of a man to contact for my own brand of equipment, and had a fascinating visit to their factory. The workers operate in conditions that are primitive compared to standards in this country, but there was certainly nothing wrong with the goods they produced.

The international began at 9.30 on a misty morning, on a pitch which looked like marble. It was rock hard, and we imagined it would be very fast, but in fact it turned out to be a beauty for batting on. We were beaten with an over to spare, having failed to make enough runs despite a powerful knock from Mike Gatting, who hit four sixes in one over. I was intrigued by the prize money: when we won the first international, in Ahmedabad, we were told afterwards that no money was awarded for the winners; this time, much to our surprise, India's captain stepped forward to pick up a cheque for 35,000 rupees – around £2000.

Given the choice between a night in a hotel near Jullundur and an overnight coach journey, we chose the coach. The trip took eight hours twenty minutes (I know the exact time because we ran a sweepstake on it), but it passed remarkably quickly since we were absorbed in card games and buoyed up by the copious supplies of beer and food on board. It was 2.30 a.m. when we pulled into the forecourt of the Oberoi Intercontinental at Delhi, but we all felt it was worth the long journey and late night for the day off which stretched before us.

The Delhi Test was played over the Christmas period, with Christmas Day itself as the rest-day. If we were to retain a chance of winning this series, we knew a victory was essential either here or in Calcutta in the Test which followed a week later. On the previous visit under Tony Greig England had won at both grounds, so we set off with recent history, at least, in our favour. Sadly, this Third Test became a faithful copy of the Second. We again batted first and began well. Boycott and I were mildly upset by a change of ball after 11 overs, for instead of substituting the faulty ball with one that had had the same amount of use, the umpires brought out a rosy new one and merely sandpapered off a little of the shine. This, of course, left the ball at its hardest; it also swung appreciably and we were forced to go through the careful playing-in process all over again. Despite this, our stand was well into three figures, and I had made 71, when I played my first stroke of any real ambition and found myself caught at mid-wicket off the inside edge. We ended the day on 190 for one – not as well advanced as we would have liked.

The next morning, Christmas Eve, we were presented to Mrs Gandhi before play resumed. I was standing at the end of the line next to Geoff Boycott, who whispered to me that he intended to give the Prime Minister a copy of his latest book, with the passage on page 203 relating to his views on South African apartheid heavily underlined. This he duly did, but Mrs Gandhi produced the perfect riposte. 'I will accept your book,' she said, 'because you caused me so much trouble before the tour!'

An unwelcome Christmas Eve visitor to the dressing-room was a rat, who scurried about the floor and gave us the improbable treat of seeing Both leap on to a bench, wielding his jumbo bat as a weapon. I have to confess I joined him.

Boycott and Tavare both made centuries that day. For Geoff it was just the latest in the line – the previous day he had broken the all-time record for Test match runs – but for Chris it was a first, hopefully of many. It seemed at one stage that we would score no more runs than on the opening day, and when Ian Botham went in with forty minutes left Fletch told him just to play normally until stumps. Ian's response to that instruction was to hit four sixes and try to smash every bowler out of the ground. It took us to 427 for four by the close of a day in which India had bowled only 11 overs an hour, hardening my belief that legislation must now be brought in to lay down a minimum number of overs per day or a penalty if the required number is not completed. The West Indies' over-rate seems slow enough, but at least they have the excuse of four pace bowlers coming off long runs. India were, for some time, operating with spin at each end, but it did not prevent Gavaskar using every means at his disposal to hold up play.

Christmas Day on tour can be a lonely and depressing time, but this year it was relieved for me by the knowledge that Brenda had packed and was ready to fly out. It was also relieved by a hilarious fancy dress party, the theme of which was 'My Hero'. I went as the soccer player Billy Bonds, although the non-arrival of the West Ham shirt I had asked Brenda to send out rather took the edge off my costume. My room-mate John Emburey went as a member of the Ku Klux Klan, Geoff Boycott went as

Ranji and Ian Botham as Geoff Boycott, complete with his total of Test runs written across his bare chest.

It was a most convivial day, but it could not inspire us to victory the day after. We batted on for much of the third morning, reaching 476 for nine, and for some while we retained a real hope of being able to make India follow on. Early on the fourth day they still wanted 90 runs with five wickets down, but the pitch was just too good. Kirmani and Shastri batted sensibly and well, and the rest was anti-climactic.

We finished the year still one down. Keith Fletcher was still waiting for his first win as England's captain, while Ian Botham was perhaps waiting to produce his next miracle. I was waiting and wondering what 1982 held in store. The year behind me had begun and ended well, with runs and confidence flowing freely. But in between lay a minefield of mixed emotions, explosive incidents, highs and lows. It had been a year of contrasts – a year I shall never forget.

The Year in Figures

England in the West Indies

First Test: Trinidad, 13–17 February
West Indies won by an innings and 79 runs
West Indies 426–9 declared; England 178 and 169
Gooch's scores: 41 and 5

Second Test: Guyana, 28 February–5 March
Cancelled

Third Test: Barbados, 13–18 March
West Indies won by 298 runs
West Indies 265 (Lloyd 100) and 379–7 declared
  (Richards 182*)
England 122 and 224 (Gooch 116)
Gooch's scores: 26 and 116

Fourth Test: Antigua, 27 March–1 April
Match drawn
England 271 (Willey 102*) and 234–3 (Boycott 104*)
West Indies 468–9 declared (Richards 114)
Gooch's scores 33 and 83

Fifth Test: Jamaica, 10–15 April
Match drawn
England 285 (Gooch 153) and 302–6 declared (Gower
  154*)
West Indies 442
Gooch's scores: 153 and 3

West Indies win series 2–0

174

England v. Australia

First Test: Trent Bridge, 18–22 June
Australia won by four wickets
England 185 and 125 (Lillee 5–46, Alderman 5–62)
Australia 179 and 132–6
Gooch's scores: 10 and 6

Second Test: Lords, 2–7 July
Match drawn
England 311 (Lawson 7–81) and 265–8 declared
Australia 345 and 90–4
Gooch's scores: 44 and 20

Third Test: Leeds, 16–21 July
England won by 18 runs
England 174 and 356 (Botham 149*, Alderman 6–135)
Australia 401–9 declared (Dyson 102, Botham 6–95) and
    111 (Willis 8–43)
Gooch's scores: 2 and 0

Fourth Test: Birmingham, 30 July–3 August
England won by 29 runs
England 189 (Alderman 5–42) and 219 (Bright 5–68)
Australia 258 and 121 (Botham 5–11)
Gooch's scores: 21 and 21

Fifth Test: Manchester, 13–17 August
England won by 103 runs
England 231 and 404 (Botham 118, Alderman 5–109)
Australia 130 and 402 (Yallop 114, Border 123*)
Gooch's scores: 10 and 5

Sixth Test: The Oval, 27 August–1 September
Match drawn
Australia 352 (Border 106*, Botham 6–125) and 344–9
    declared (Wellham 103)
England 314 (Boycott 137, Lillee 7–89) and 261–7
Gooch did not play

---

* denotes not out score

175

Gooch in County Cricket

County Championship averages:
Batting: 9 matches, 17 innings, 1091 runs, average: 64.17
 Centuries (5): 164 v. Leicestershire, 146 v. Northants,
 122 v. Somerset, 113 v. Glamorgan,
 105 v. Leicestershire
Bowling: 63 overs, 20 maidens, 181 runs, 5 wickets,
 average: 36.20

Essex positions:
Schweppes County Championship – 5th
Benson & Hedges Cup – failed to reach last 8
NatWest Bank Trophy – semifinalists
John Player League – Champions

India Tour, 1981–82

First Test: Bombay, 27 November–2 December
India won by 132 runs
India 179 and 227
England 166 and 102
Gooch's scores: 2 and 1

Second Test: Bangalore, 9–14 December
Match drawn
England 400 and 174–3
India 428
Gooch's scores: 58 and 40

Third Test: Delhi, 23–28 December
Match drawn
England 476–9 declared and 68–0
India 487
Gooch's scores: 71 and 20*

Fourth Test: Calcutta, 1–6 January
Match drawn
England 248 and 265–5
India 208 and 170–3
Gooch's scores: 47 and 63

Fifth Test: Madras, 13–18 January
Match drawn
India 481–4 declared and 160–3
England 328
Gooch's score: 127

Sixth Test: Kanpur, 30 January–4 February
Match drawn
England 378–9 declared
India 377–7
Gooch's score: 58

Gooch's tour Test averages
10 innings (1 not out), 487 runs
average: 54.11